CW00553946

A Thousand Fancies

The Collection of Charles Wade of Snowshill Manor

Acknowledgements

This book owes a debt of gratitude to the late Michael Jessop, whose compilation of Wade's own work, interviews with those who knew him, and own further research have shaped our understanding of Wade, the manor and its collection since the 1980s. My research has further benefited from National Trust archives, National Archives (UK), St Christopher National Trust and the Government Archives of St Kitts and Nevis. Among the many individuals who have assisted me I would especially like to thank David Adshead, the publishing team at National Trust, Jenny Rowley-Bowen and the staff at Snowshill Manor, Hazel Brookes and Yolunde Dunn for their research assistance, Thenford Grey for his expertise as a guide to St Kitts, and Helene Lucas for her hospitality at the White House. I am most grateful to Simon Houfe for his knowledge, generosity and admittance into the magical world of Sir Albert Richardson, and to Viki O'Flaherty for her encouragement and unwavering research assistance in St Kitts. Finally, I would like to thank Sally for her support and sound judgement.

Jonathan Howard

The National Trust gratefully acknowledges a generous bequest from the late Mr and Mrs Kenneth Levy that has supported the cost of preparing this book.

First published 2016

The History Press
The Mill, Brimscombe Port, Stroud, Gloucestershire, GL5 2QG
www.thehistorypress.co.uk

© National Trust 2016
Text © Jonathan Howard 2016

The right of Jonathan Howard to be identified as the Author of this work has been asserted in accordance with the Copyright, Designs and Patents Act 1988.

All images © National Trust, except for: *Country Life*: p.5.

All rights reserved. No part of this book may be reprinted or reproduced or utilised in any form or by any electronic, mechanical or other means, now known or hereafter invented, including photocopying and recording, or in any information storage or retrieval system, without the permission in writing from the Publishers.
British Library Cataloguing in Publication Data.
A catalogue record for this book is available from the British Library.

ISBN 978-1-84165-675-5

Design by Katie Beard
Printed in China

Contents

Charles's cottage kitchen at Snowshill Manor in the early 1920s.

Charles Wade outside
Snowshill Manor in
the early 1920s.

Introduction

In 1918, whilst serving on the Western Front, in a canteen in Doullens, Charles Paget Wade came across an old property supplement for *Country Life* magazine. Here he saw a photograph of the 'old Cotswold Manor House' which stood at the centre of the village of Snowshill in the north-west corner of Gloucestershire. This moment would alter the course of his life. The manor was being auctioned off as part of the Snowshill Manor Estate, and the advertisement was dated 17 June 1916. Although likely sold long since, Charles was captivated and determined, if he lived to see England again, to seek Snowshill Manor out and make it his own.

He did, creating a terraced Arts and Crafts garden inside its stone walls, and repairing, restoring and altering the manor house to host a unique collection of craftsmanship. Since 1952 the National Trust has opened Snowshill Manor to visitors – now over 80,000 a year. Here, cast in shadow, visitors see boneshakers, mangles and serpents. Modelled in half-light are Balinese masks, Armada chests and a Noah's Ark. In the heavens, cherubs, flying foxes and model ships are in suspense. Time has many faces in the manor, and finishes abound in gold, vermilion and ancient grained woods. Today more than 22,000 objects of craftsmanship rest here, collected through seven decades of Charles's life, and arranged in 22 rooms in a manner reminiscent of his provocative and imaginative ways.

Visitors catch sight of his strange likenesses in the guidebook, in leaflets and on the web. He is thin, just under five-and-a-half-feet tall, long in the trunk and short in the bandy leg. His swarthy face is long and lined, eyes dark and sparkling framed by tortoiseshell-rimmed glasses set on high cheek bones under a strong, furrowed brow. His hair is thick, long, curled just below the line of the ears, as one might expect of a puritan of the 17th century. Before the war he had lived a bohemian lifestyle as an architect on the Hampstead Garden Suburb, where the inhabitants were regarded as 'crazy, crankish, freakish people', and 'Men wore their hair long; girls wore it short'. Even in these circles Charles was described as 'one of the most colourful', and noted for 'unparalleled eccentricity and bohemian dress'. After the war he was commonly seen in a winged collar, with bow tie, dark waistcoat, single-breasted wool jacket and matching knee breeches, met by ribbed woollen socks rising from his leather brogues.

At the time he was called up Charles had renounced architecture to become an artist and illustrator, and was living an increasingly free and creative lifestyle, supported by the luxury of financial independence, derived principally from sugar-cane plantations in the West Indies. With his comfortable means he chose not to live at the forefront of contemporary fashion, but instead detached himself from it. For inspiration and

NOTICE OF AUCTION.
On Wednesday, June 21st, at Broadway, Worcs.

THE SNOWSHILL MANOR ESTATE.
SNOWSHILL, near Broadway, Worcs, in eight lots, including a fine OLD COTSWOLD MANOR HOUSE, as illustrated above, and 215 acres, a capital Hill Farm and 246 acres, a Tudor Cottage Residence and five acres, and several old cottages capable of conversion into week-end cottages.— Illustrated particulars from G. H. BAYLEY & SONS, 4, Promenade, Cheltenham.

The *Country Life* advert for Snowshill Manor.

A 17th-century Armada chest, now in Zenith.

style he was naturally drawn to the 17th and 18th centuries. Like many others he did not volunteer to fight; he did not want to relinquish the lifestyle he had determinedly created and cherished. He saw military service, as he regarded school, as a regime that set out to control, forcing conformity, and so he tried to avoid it.

Once compelled into military service, he appeared to have no choice; his appearance was 'standardised'. His long hair was cut short and his archaic attire replaced with khaki. Yet Charles's characteristic determination to control his surroundings showed through the regulation, serge and mud. Posted as an orderly room clerk for a section of the Third Army Workshop Company, in an Armstrong hut 16 feet x 6 feet, during the evenings he set about to make this 'canvas shack' look 'quite attractive'. He lined the interior with 'sand bag' hessian, built 'neat shelves and a cupboard for army papers', hung 'a few pictures', and made a 'pleasing cover' for his bunk. His officer, Second Lieutenant William Wildman Tweedy, was impressed but also concerned about the reaction it might produce in his superiors, saying, 'I think, Wade, we ought to have some Army maps about in case a General comes; this place looks too comfortable for a war!' Charles duly added the maps but his sensibilities also required him to add frames and hand colouring to avoid detracting from the ambience and 'cosiness of the room'. Even he was surprised when a visiting general congratulated him on the effect he had achieved with 'so little at hand'.

In the years that followed Charles transformed Snowshill Manor and welcomed increasing numbers of visitors, guiding them around his catholic collection of craftsmanship. Some remarked on how nimble he was, and his ability to move with unnatural silence; that as he handled objects his hands were strong but precise, and his voice crackled as he spoke of their provenance and former use. He became something of a celebrity, known very well by very few, and not well by thousands more. Queen Mary, visiting Snowshill, reputedly judged him the most remarkable object in his collection. When Charles died his old friend the Conservative MP Christopher Holland-Martin described him, as others have before and since, as 'one of the true English Eccentrics'. Over half a century after his death 'eccentric' and 'quirky' are still the words most commonly applied to him, and, based on Snowshill Manor alone, this judgement is understandable.

In many ways the outward expression of his inward beliefs and values do fit the characteristics of an eccentric. For example, psychologist David Weeks states these characteristics as nonconformist, creative, idealistic, enjoying an intense curiosity and a happy obsession with hobbies, being aware in early childhood that they are different from others, highly intelligent, opinionated, outspoken, having a lack of interest in opinions or company of others, having unusual living or eating habits, exhibiting a mischievous sense of humour.

Apt as this description may be, one must take into account other aspects of Charles's character. On the one hand, the term 'eccentric' may popularly connote a whimsical and quirky personality unaware of social norms. This is certainly not a true likeness of Charles. His attitude to the family business and to money was respectful

View across the gardens of the manor house and cottage at Snowshill.

Left: Javanese and Balinese theatre masks in Seraphim.
Below: A close-up view of a wooden Noah's Ark from the mid-19th century, now in Seventh Heaven.

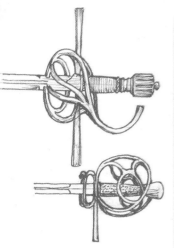

Right: Virginia Woolf, who visited Snowshill Manor.
Below: A brass spit jack that Charles bought in 1906.

and, in spite of his prodigious collecting, prudent. Reading his business letters, telegrams and board minutes it would be easy to visualise a man quite at odds with the one who created Snowshill Manor, but, like the family business, Snowshill was the result of deliberate thought and action rather than whimsy.

On the other hand, it may imply someone who is too aware of the world's opinion, whose lifestyle is all for show. Virginia Woolf labelled him a 'fraud'. But the values Charles lived by were genuine and consistent, and his reputation for eccentricity was their product rather than their object. From childhood his imagination and romantic tendencies quite naturally drew him back in time and held him there as Victorian and Edwardian society rapidly advanced. This set him further and further apart from his contemporaries, who came to see him as a relic from a previous century. Charles's archaic values were evidenced in every aspect of his life, not merely his outward appearance, though he was never so naive or militant as to try to abandon the 20th century entirely. He used cars and buses to expedite his search for antiques whilst celebrating the design and craftsmanship of coach- and wagon-making. He abhorred the destruction of interior atmospheres through electrical lighting but used battery power to create surprises at Snowshill, and did not boycott electricity elsewhere.

But consciously or unconsciously, the term 'eccentric' can serve to belittle or dismiss Charles's determination and achievements, and foreclose any effort to delve more deeply into his values and motivations. His championship of the skill and beauty of individual handcrafted objects of former times is summed up in his self-proclaimed motto: *Ne quid pereat* – 'let nothing perish'.

His interest in these objects was not only about preservation, though. He valued them

for the joy of their discovery, for the stories they told, and their power to provoke a unique imaginative response – to work together to produce a theatrical experience. His celebration of craftsmanship and desire to create total environments were rooted in childhood imagination but shaped by study, training and careful reflection. Though he gave up practising architecture before the war, he continued to identify as a member of this profession throughout his life. He was also a respected painter and illustrator, and a highly skilled craftsman and modeller. In his later years he increasingly set down his values in writing.

As time has passed and his friends have died, these facets of his work have become obscured by his most conspicuous legacy. While Snowshill Manor and its collection is the culmination of his imaginative view of the world, it cannot properly be understood without the perspective of his life, values and other achievements.

Note: Any quoted words and passages have been taken from the various writings of Charles Wade himself; these works are detailed in the Bibliography.

An incomplete watercolour of a fair by Charles, painted whilst serving in France in 1918.

Ancestral Voices 1725–1883

Charles Wade left selective information for posterity about his immediate family. Assisted by the investigative efforts of his friend, the author Kate Murray, he produced two notebooks called the *Book of Wade* and the *Book of Bulwer* which discuss and theorise about his ancestry.

The *Book of Bulwer* included a great deal of information about the Bulwer and Spencer families provided by his mother, grandmother and great-grandmother. In the *Book of Wade* Charles did not recount the history of his nearest Wade ancestors; rather ignoring them for more romantic ancestral possibilities which, without a chain of evidence leading back from the present, were little more than speculation. Armagil Waad or Armigill Wade, Chief Clerk to the Privy Council of Henry VIII, 'the English Columbus', was a historical figure Charles focused on as a potential ancestor. This connection may have been an unwritten family story passed down, since in the 1920s Charles's mother was also interested in him. Charles made a point of staking a claim to Armagil and his son, painting their coats of arms and hanging them in the Entrance Hall at Snowshill Manor, but no verification of this family connection has so far

A turtleshell shield painted with a coat of arms.

been unearthed. Whilst he records various Wades as living on or near St Kitts in the West Indies from the 17th century, any link to them is purely conjecture; he was unable to provide any evidence of a relationship between these Wades and the earliest of his ancestors, and the ancestor he describes as having arrived on the neighbouring island of St Martin in the 1770s is unnamed.

The book's omission of recent Wade family history might result from lack of information, though this would be surprising given that there were then still two Wade aunts living, along with his mother, who had married into the family. Perhaps Charles was uninterested – or felt that the identity and origins of the Wades were better left unstated. However, to understand Charles Paget Wade and Snowshill Manor, which ultimately defined him, it is necessary to remedy this omission and give an account of both sides of the family. It is the Wade side that can be credited for the wealth into which he was born and which enabled his later life of independent means. The Leeward Islands, and particularly St Kitts, were inextricably linked to the rising status of the family and Charles's destiny, and ongoing management of the business interests there was to be a continuing focus throughout his later life.

Charles's great-great-great-grandparents, the Revd John Paget (b.*c*.1670) and his wife Ann, of Egham, Surrey, are the earliest known ancestors on this side of the family. Their fourth child Thomas Paget (b.1725) was educated at Eton and King's College, Cambridge. He returned to Egham as rector of the parish church before leaving England for health reasons, arriving in St Kitts in the West Indies by 1758, with his wife Mary. Thomas and Mary had seven

children in the next ten years (Ann Cleland, John Langley, Mary Nicholls, Elizabeth Nolan, Jane, Thomas and Frances). It has previously been thought that Jane gave birth to Charles's great-grandfather, Abraham Solomon Wade. In fact, Jane married Giles Mardenbrough, a plantation owner on the nearby island of St Martin. This brought her youngest sister Frances into contact with Abraham, also of St Martin, who was a widower and previously married to Ruth Mardenbrough, Giles's sister. Frances and Abraham, Charles's great-grandparents, married in 1791 and had six children: Ann Maria Paget, Elizabeth Frances, Ann Garvey, Jane Mardenbrough, Elizabeth Taylor and Solomon Abraham. After Abraham's death Frances and her children moved to St Kitts.

It is evident from later slave registers and wills that Abraham and Frances were financially well established. The extent to which this wealth was inherited from their respective families or improved upon is unclear; it is not currently known where the Wades came from before their arrival in St Martin. Like the Paget sisters' before them, though, the marriages of the daughters of Abraham and Frances were to further their connections within the landed classes of St Kitts.

SOLOMON WADE: SOWING THE FAMILY FORTUNE

The only known son of Abraham and Frances, Solomon Abraham Wade – Charles's grandfather – was born in 1806. He first appears in records in 1831 as the

A painting of St Kitts by Charles Wade.

Paget, Wade and Bulwer Family Tree

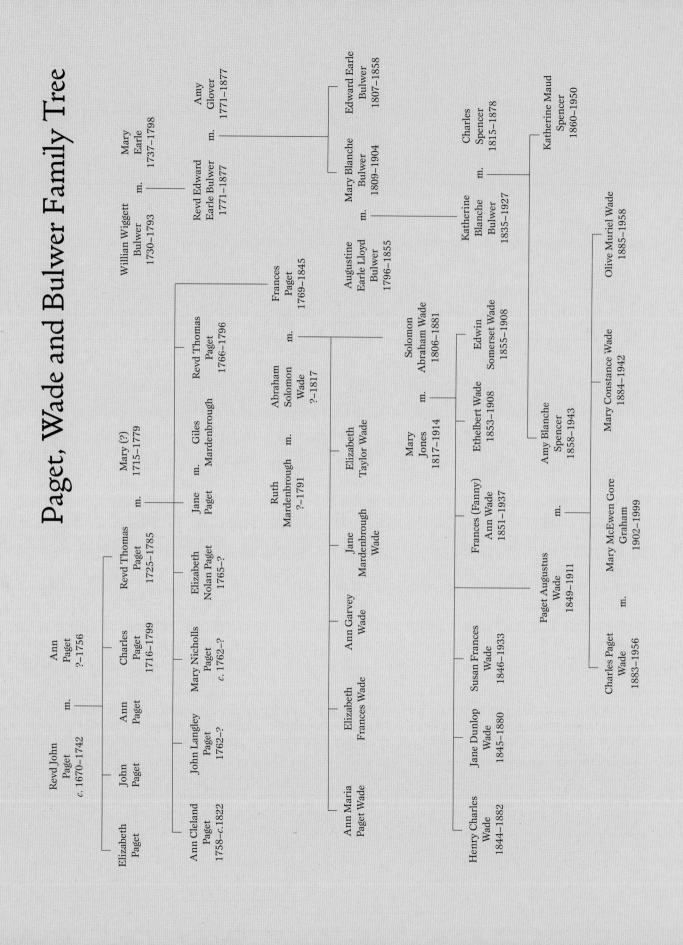

owner of two slaves, Trouble (29 years old, originally from the Congo) and Charles (four years old, originally from St Martin), both gifted to him by his mother, Frances. In 1834 Solomon no longer had these slaves, but registered a new one, Robert, who was a mere two years and eight months old and was freed on 1 August that year as a result of the Slavery Abolition Act of 1833. By this time Solomon had established himself as a merchant in St Kitts, focusing his mercantile operations on its various ports and settlements.

By 1843 Solomon was in a relationship with Mary Jones (1817–1914), Charles's grandmother. Mary, born in St Kitts, was black and appears to have been born free rather than being a slave. There is no evidence to show how she met Solomon, but she is reputed to have been his housekeeper. However, when Mary gave birth to Solomon's first child, Henry Charles Wade, on 30 March 1844 she was recorded as being employed as a huckster.

Sometime in 1845 another child was born, Jane Dunlop. Susan Frances was born in 1846. By the time Paget Augustus, Charles Wade's father, was born, in January 1849, Mary was recorded as working as a seamstress. Frances (Fanny) Ann was born in 1851, followed by Ethelbert in 1853 and Edwin Somerset in 1855. Nine months prior to Edwin's birth, on 30 January 1855, Solomon Wade had finally married Mary Jones, at St Thomas's, on the west side of the Island.

Why Solomon (assuming it was his decision) waited so long is unknown, since interracial marriages were not rare in the colonies. Perhaps as his wealth increased he was able to re-evaluate the level to which he could rise commercially and socially. By the time of his marriage Solomon had established a partnership with his trusted employee Samuel Abbott to strengthen his merchant business. Wade and Abbott

A group of plantation workers in St Kitts.

became agents for owners of estates and it is clear that Solomon gained a good understanding of the sugar industry and which estates had the greatest potential. In 1850 Solomon had purchased his first plantation, Bakers, marking a major shift in the emphasis of his commercial expansion. Nine years later he bought College and Pensez-if-bien, later known as Douglas Estates. It is with the purchase of Douglas that Solomon gained ownership of the White House, which was to be a family home in St Kitts for the next 110 years, and significant in Charles's own later life. It is said that Solomon brought out a team of Italian gardeners to create the garden while builders restored and improved the house. Over the next few years Solomon would acquire Bayfords and Blois, and the Hermitage Estates, his increasing landholdings matched by a growing profile in society. In 1855 he may have felt that 'living in sin' could prove an obstacle to realising his potential.

The decision to marry may also have been prompted by a plan to move the family to England, as many other St Kitts landowners did.

The Red Lion in Basseterre, St Kitts.

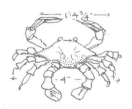

By 1861 Solomon had sent his wife and six of their children to live at Belmont Hill, Kent. The eldest daughter, Jane, for obscure reasons, stayed behind in St Kitts. Paget joined other sons of wealthy St Kitts planters at Totteridge Park Grammar School in Hertfordshire, before moving up to King's College School in the Strand. Solomon was not intimidated by the unconventional position his family would occupy in Victorian society, and rather than hide them away in St Kitts was comfortable to set them up in England, to give them a higher standard of education and living. Nonetheless, Charles's father and aunts and uncles were illegitimate, of mixed race and born into trade. In this is a possible explanation for Charles's – or his relatives' – reticence to record recent Wade family history.

Solomon himself remained in St Kitts until late 1868, when he moved permanently to England, visiting St Kitts annually from then on. The eldest son, Henry Charles, had previously returned to St Kitts to learn the family business and enter the partnership of Wade and Abbott. Between 1868 and 1871 Solomon lived at Point House, Attleborough, in Norfolk, England, where he was joined by Mary and their two daughters while the three younger boys boarded in London. The attraction of Attleborough may have been that it was an ancestral stamping ground: there are Wades recorded as living in Attleborough,

and others in the surrounding villages of Buckenham and the Ellinghams.

MEETING THE SPENCERS

During the years in Attleborough the Wade family made the acquaintance of the Revd Charles Spencer, curate of the parish. Spencer was educated at Pembroke College, Cambridge, before becoming the curate of Cawston by 1843, where he assisted the rector of the parish, Augustine Earle Lloyd Bulwer. Augustine had married his cousin, Mary Blanche Bulwer, and one of their daughters was Katherine Blanche. Charles Spencer formed an attachment with Katherine, and they married the year after Augustine died. Given the high status of the Bulwer family, Charles does not seem to be an ambitious match for Katherine, and one might be tempted to read significance into the marriage taking place after her father's death, and in London. However, it is clear that Augustine became well acquainted with Charles before his death and the fact

that his wife Mary remained very close to her daughter and grandchildren after the marriage shows at the very least an acceptance of the union. Perhaps it helped that both she and her son-in-law were musical. She played the pianoforte and Charles, like her father Revd Edward Earle Bulwer, played the flute.

After their marriage Charles and Katherine moved to Wherstead Grove, near Ipswich, where their eldest daughter, Amy Blanche Spencer, was born in 1858. Later that year Charles became the curate at Great and Little Ellingham in Norfolk and the family came to live in Attleborough. The black clerical robes he inherited from the previous curate remain in the Snowshill collection.

Charles and Katherine's second daughter (Katherine) Maud was born at Attleborough in 1860. Her elder sister Amy was full of fun, drawing and dressing as a brave in 'Indian things', painting her face, arms and legs, and running about the field. Her childhood interests seem to herald those of

An imaginary English market town square, painted by Charles Wade in 1910.

The Music Room at Snowshill Manor.

her son, Charles, who at the same age would write about how he and his sisters built a hut based on an Indian one he had seen in a children's book.

Katherine Spencer's journal entry for 1 November 1866 records that she and her husband ('Charlie') attended a concert in Norwich with a 'Miss Wade', and one may infer her esteem from the pairing of this name with that of the Duke of Edinburgh who was also in attendance. Katherine now regularly socialised and went riding with the Miss Wades until, in 1871, both families left Attleborough. The Wades set up home in Anerley, Surrey. The Spencers first took up a curacy in Lancashire, and then moved to a new posting near Worcester in 1872.

Despite this separation the Wades and Spencers continued their intimacy. Paget, by now a partner in Wade and Abbott, was a visitor. Twelve-year-old Amy writes about

her future husband for the first time in June 1870 in a letter to her grandmother ('Gan'):

Paget Wade has brought home such a dear little monkey, his name is Jacko, he is full of tricks and if I hold a piece of sugar in my hand and shut it up he will open it to find the sugar.

Paget has also brought home a Parrot, it is green with red above the beak and yellow in the tail and wings, it cannot talk. Mr Wade gave us a piece of sugar cane and some oranges as big as my head! They are very nice, much better than we can buy. We did not think much of the sugar, as it was very chaffy.

Over the next few years the Wades and Spencers continued to visit and stay with each other. On 21 September 1878, however, Charles Spencer died.

Charles (left) looking on as estate manager Arthur Evelyn speaks to workers at Mansion Estate, St Kitts, c.1933.

WADE FORTUNES

Although Solomon had retired to England he continued to acquire estates in St Kitts. By 1878 he owned College, Douglas, 'Pogson's Cayon', Dalzell's, Losack's, Lavington's, Canada, Key Estates, Upper and Lower Spooners Cayon Estates and Golden Rock Estates. He had earlier sold Bayfords and Blois. Given the number of estates Solomon possessed it can be considered significant that he chose to remain known as 'merchant', rather than a landowner and planter. He perhaps felt that this was more fitting for his operations and outlook – and had fewer negative social connotations than those associated with the title 'planter'.

These years were also marked by Solomon's concerted efforts to establish his four sons. He sold Canada Estate to Henry, who was living at the White House, commenting that he was 'very lucky for now he has a fine Estate with water and new machinery, he ought to derive a good income from the property'. The fourth son,

Edwin, had been articled to a QC as a legal clerk for five years in 1873, but returned to St Kitts after two. Solomon wanted Edwin to return to England to study agriculture before coming back to manage an estate in St Kitts, but Edwin stayed on as a planter at Douglas Estate, giving his father grounds for grave concerns about his judgement and self-discipline. His brother Ethelbert trained to become a medical doctor but never graduated. By comparison with Henry and Paget, Ethelbert and Edwin underachieved, perhaps for reasons suggested by their later causes of death: cirrhosis of the liver and neurosyphilis respectively.

In November 1879 Solomon wrote to Paget to let him know how he had arranged matters for him:

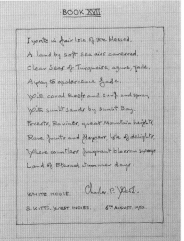

The frontispiece of Volume 17 of Charles's handwritten notebooks.

You will find in reading my will dated this day that your name is not included therein as a beneficiary except you are forgiven a sum due from you to me and are to participate in the Residue Estate. The reason is that I have made you a present of £16,000 to enable you to purchase of Messrs. Bosanquet and Curtis, the Mansion Estate in the West Indies.

After taking possession of Mansion Estate, Paget purchased the adjoining Woodleys Estate in 1880. He then combined these estates with Rose Hill and Bakers Estate to form 807 acres known as Mansion Estate. The original Mansion Estate, with its big house, became known as Upper Mansion and this is where Paget was to stay when he visited the island.

Unlike Henry and Edwin, Paget was committed to residing in England. From 1871 he worked in partnership with Neville Catlyn Sendall in a new company called

The Spencer family in 1877: Revd Charles Spencer and Mrs Katherine Spencer are seated; standing behind are their daughters, Katherine Maud and Amy Blanche Spencer, Charles Wade's mother.

Sendall and Wade, based in London. The partnership focused on importing Wade and associates' produce from the West Indies and selling it on the British market. Being both the producer in St Kitts and the agent selling the sugar in England maximised the Wades' profits and was not an uncommon model.

It is unclear whether it was Paget's preference to be based in England, or if he simply complied with a wider plan engineered by Solomon to strengthen and expand the family business. There is no doubt that Paget was fond of his birthplace, however, and he was always quick to rally to any emergency faced by St Kitts or the other Leeward Islands, organising relief from floods, hurricanes and famine.

The years 1880 to 1882 were marked by three sad losses for the Wade family. First, on Christmas Eve 1880 Jane Dunlop, Solomon's eldest daughter, died in St Kitts. Next, Solomon himself was struck down in February 1881 whilst on his annual visit to St Kitts and was bedridden for two weeks. In a letter he told Paget that he was suffering 'from the effect of a chigoe [a tropical flea] having made its way in my left foot, which caused an inflammation and was much swollen with fever'. Solomon managed to return to England in April, but he never recovered from the illness and eventually succumbed to complications on 17 August 1881 at his home. In his last will he bequeathed much of his property to his eldest child, Henry; he gave Hermitage Estate to Ethelbert, and to Edwin, the College, Douglas and Green Estates. He also cancelled the outstanding debts Paget owed to him, as promised.

Henry seems to have had a close relationship with Solomon, and he himself died at the White House on 5 October 1882, aged 38, in mysterious circumstances. It appears that he had returned from England a few days before his death, and whilst physically well his friends noted that he 'had

THE · COURTYARD   · S · KITTS ·

All white and Green - all green and white,
A Gallery to Left and Right
Green Jalousies and White wood walls,
'Neath Shingle Roof deep shadow falls.
In centre is a wide stone stair
To Galleries, from Garden fair.
Tall Cinnamon with leaves deep green,
And glowing stems with silken sheen.
'Oer Gallery climbs purple wreath
With Stephanotis underneath.
Many a fragrant petal rare
Sheds sweetest scents upon the Air.

Prospect afar o'er BASSETERRE Bay
NEVIS in haze there fades away.
White gleams a wall by ancient Pier,
White Schooner and small Sloops lie there.

25 · 8 · 48

manifested symptoms of an unsound mind'; he was suffering from melancholy which had caused the 'greatest anxiety' to them. His death certificate recorded that he died of arsenic poisoning, and it was reported that he killed himself either through misadventure or intentionally. Perhaps Henry was unhinged by his father's recent death, but there were also complications in his personal life. Upon Henry's death Paget moved decisively to assume the mantle vacated by his older brother, purchasing a 50 per cent interest in the partnership of Wade and Abbott. The business concerns that Henry had accumulated with those he inherited from his father were now returned to the family, on whose behalf Paget took over their management. Each brother still retained the ownership of his own personal estates.

Happier times came in the form of Paget's marriage to Amy Blanche Spencer, on 18 April 1882. It is unclear how long the couple had been engaged, though the marriage and their affections had been years in the making. Given that Paget was of mixed race and 'in trade', the match may have raised some eyebrows among the genteel relatives of Amy's mother. Yet the two families clearly had a longstanding friendship, and perhaps Katherine Spencer's own experience of marrying for love overrode other social sensibilities – though the Wades' wealth might do this equally well.

A poem from one of Charles's notebooks about the White House and courtyard in St Kitts.

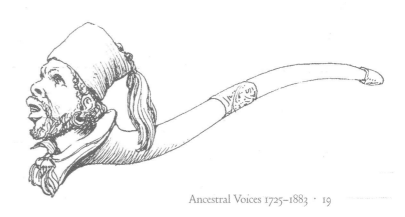

2 Seventh Heaven and Hades 1883–1901

Immediately after their wedding, Amy and Paget moved into a house called Arthog (renamed Birchwood a couple of years later) at Shortlands – not far from the Wades' family home, St Martins. So happy were they there that almost nine months to the day after their wedding, Charles Paget Wade was born on 13 February 1883. His first name was given in recognition of his grandfather Spencer and, perhaps more, of his recently deceased uncle Henry Charles Wade, who had been known as 'Charlie'. His middle name, like his father's first name, dated back to Revd Thomas Paget.

Soon after the birth Paget travelled to St Kitts to inspect the family estates and meet with business contacts and employees, returning to England in early April. It is evident that his absences were felt, and made for productive homecomings. Nine months after his return Amy gave birth to Mary Constance ('Connie') on 10 February 1884. Similarly, nine months after his homecoming in April 1884 Olive Muriel was born on 19 February 1885. After Olive's birth Paget consolidated this yearly travel routine that he and later his wife Amy and son Charles would follow for the rest of their lives, of departing England for St Kitts between November and February and returning to England in April/May.

Charles Wade's sisters, *c*.1889: Olive Muriel (above) and Constance (Connie) (below). *Below, right:* Charles and Connie as children, *c*.1887.

THIS HAPPY REALM: EARLY CHILDHOOD

Although very close to his parents, their absence from Charles's life only made him more self-sufficient and resourceful. Through his early childhood he inhabited what he described as 'the underworld'. This 'happy realm' existed across the floor, under furniture and in cupboards. Here his toys played out games and adventures across 'the ribs of floorboard's grain' and 'the Persian rug's soft velvet feel'. He loved the nursery at Birchwood. Here, every spare space was full of the toys in which he 'found comfort and friendship'. At night, lying in bed, he would watch the firelight create provocative, animated shapes on the nursery walls and ceiling.

Throughout his life Charles was fascinated by shops – how the stock was arranged and what he might discover in them. As a child he loved the confectioner's, unsurprisingly, but later wrote that the toy shop 'most certainly is the best shop of all, for all fantasy reigns, all poor human limitations are swept away, nothing is impossible'. A favourite toy was the greengrocer's shop manned by 'Robert', whose imaginary business flourished so much that Charles had to build him a larger counter to replace the short original one. Robert made deliveries in the furniture van with the 'bewildering' word *Pantechnicon* written across it. In the van, pulled by a pair of dapple-grey horses, Robert would 'take three or four somewhat reckless drives round the nursery returning to the same house to unload'. His mother's doll's house was another favourite. It was in the Queen Anne style, built of red brick with white sash windows and a 'wide friendly door of emerald green with a brass lion knocker'.

Charles later wrote of childhood Christmases with great nostalgia, and mentioned especially the excitement that built up in the week before. There were

Charles Wade aged seven.

trips to the shop kept by Miss Faulds and her 'crazy mother' with the red wig, and Christmas parties with the flash of carriage lamps as guests pulled up to the front door in the snow. What distinguished his experience from other children's was not just the quantity of presents, but their quality. Coming from a privileged family his presents were often on the very cutting edge of technology, and the expense and quality of these toys were not wasted on Charles's active imagination. A memorable Christmas present was Noah's Ark with pairs of wonderfully carved and painted figures. However, whilst there was no doubt that Noah was a great conservationist, Charles lost all respect for him as a shipwright when, having placed the Ark in the bath, it took on water, capsized, and drowned all within.

A particular inspiration for Charles in his formative years was Kate Greenaway's *Painting Book* and *Almanac and Language of Flowers*, and in his old age he wrote a poem to thank her for the 'worlds in which I joy to stray'. Other favourite books

Charles Wade's toy shop.

The doll's house that formerly belonged to Charles Wade's mother.

were Randolph Caldecott's *Mad Dog* and Mrs Ewing's *Daddy Darwin's Dovecote*, both illustrated by Caldecott. He believed that he was unread and gained more from observation and trial and error than from reading a book. However, there is no doubt that his art then and later was greatly influenced by the work of these illustrators.

Music, on the other hand, was neither a childhood nor adult pursuit for Charles. Despite his mother's family's interest, it does not appear that he ever learnt an instrument, though his sisters played the piano and violin. This did not deter him from accumulating a significant collection of musical instruments through his later life, as the Music Room at Snowshill shows.

Charles never knew his grandfathers, but he and his sisters often stayed with their grandmothers. Mary Wade lived until 1914, when Charles was 31, and he remembered her as 'loving and kind', like a character from a 'fairy book', sitting in her armchair with 'a large white cap on her white hair'. Mary invested hours in her grandson, listening to him and playing solitaire and marbles with him. The spiced syllabubs and egg noggins she made for him may reinforce the claim that she had once been Solomon's housekeeper. She had a great love for flowers and grew stoned fruit, pears, and 'every kind of berry'. In her garden pond Charles would sail his model boat.

At Christmas time 1890 Charles and his sisters went to stay for a week with Mary in Teddington, London. Their visit was to culminate with the Drury Lane Pantomime *Jack and the Beanstalk*. Charles was equally captivated on the trip to the theatre by the livery of the locomotive and the 'two stately footmen' of the carriage with their scarlet coats, black satin knee breeches, white silk stockings and powdered wigs. Having found their seats in the balcony, Charles divided his gaze between the sea of faces below and the 'constellation of stars piercing the domed ceiling above', and waited for the 'wondrous things to come'. A decade later he would pursue this fascination with theatre.

GRANNY SPENCER AND GREAT YARMOUTH

Katherine Spencer, Charles's other grandmother, would live until 1927, when he was 44, and his recollections of her were less glowing. Paget travelled to the West Indies for four months of the year, sometimes accompanied by Amy, so Charles, aged six, was sent to be schooled away from home, as was accepted practice. He went to live with Granny Spencer in Great Yarmouth, to attend Miss Haddon's private school nearby. From this time forth, for the remainder of his education, Charles would no longer live at home except at weekends and holidays. His sisters attended other schools but would come to visit him at Granny Spencer's now and then. Charles was very close to his sisters, especially Connie, and being away from them and his parents was difficult for him, but fortunately he had the imagination and resourcefulness to bear it.

Granny Spencer's house stood in a 'drab' street of terraced, bay brick houses built in 1822, and although the house was well proportioned he found it to be similarly drab and lonely. She lived a spartan existence characterised by plain food, hard beds and chilblains. She was strict and observed set routines which meant that 'every day was

much the same'. They both attended church twice on a Sunday, the morning at St John and evensong at St Nicholas. As a consequence of this routine lifestyle, rare trips to a church fair or circus stood out in Charles's memory. In contrast to Granny Spencer, her mother Mary, who lived just across the street, 'enjoyed a joke and was good company'. She also kept a good fire, which was a standard of lifelong importance to Charles.

Although 'drab', the house contained many objects which were not only interesting to look at but had stories that drew Charles back in time, connected him with his ancestors and inspired him. The family treasures included old silhouettes, miniatures and 18th-century furniture. Of greatest significance to him was a Cantonese shrine cabinet which Granny Spencer only allowed to be opened on Sundays. The exterior was finished in black lacquer with gold-leaf decorative overlay. Opening the double doors revealed a gilded 'heavenly Palace of faraway Cathay' with stairs leading to colonnaded and screened courtyards scented with spices. Charles would later write, 'I know nothing which can inspire such an intense Fairy Land atmosphere, as these Chinese lacquer cabinets'. Inhabiting its spaces and the numerous drawers were family curios. Here Charles saw a Russian soldier's cap badge which Granny Spencer's cousin, General Sir Edward Earle Gascoigne Bulwer, found at Balaclava whilst serving in the British Army during the Crimean War. She gave this to Charles, along with the cabinet itself and eight others like it.

The cabinet's spaces, enticing the viewer to enter, greatly influenced the interiors

A Noah's Ark.

Below: Two cut
paper silhouettes
mounted on card
depicting Edward
Bulwer in uniform.
Bottom: A music
box. According to
the handwritten
label, it plays
'"MEET ME BY
MOONLIGHT" by
Joseph Augustine
Wade. 1796–1845.'

Charles would later create at Snowshill Manor. If Snowshill is the culmination of his life, this cabinet represents the critical first step towards that; the treasures it housed and the stories they told ignited a passion for collecting which began there in Great Yarmouth. At the age of seven he bought three French shrines carved of bone for 1s 6d (today about £5), one dedicated to St Michael and the other two to the Virgin and Child. These were housed in Granny's cabinet in Snowshill until they were stolen in the 1970s.

With hindsight Charles had much to be grateful to his Granny Spencer for. He may never have agreed with this, but his life with her taught him to rely heavily on his imagination and his surroundings to inspire him. He had some independence and the sea, sailors and ships – a great source of interest for him – were close at hand. True, it was difficult to get out of the house at times. Granny's 'repulsive' garden, 'pinched between two dreary drab walls', was alleviated only by daffodils, a pigeon house and a decorative zinc meat safe. In fact, the meat safe was often a tool for Charles's incarceration: if the zinc roof was dark in appearance she would announce there was 'damp in the air' and he would have to stay indoors.

Sometimes, when he was released beyond the clutches of the house and garden, Charles met another veteran of the Crimean War, Charles Dye, who worked as a 'road mender'. In spite of living in 'a desolate, a most dismal place', he and his wife Mary-Ann had, unlike Granny, worked miracles to create an 'enticing' garden which embodied the 'charm of the country'. The Dyes gave Charles personal effects to add to his growing collection.

The daily seaside route to and from Miss Haddon's School was also a source of consolation and inspiration. En route, at the Aquarium, on the rare occasion he had money, he would set automated penny machines in motion with ships sailing stormy seas, soldiers marching, a train passing through a tunnel, or a quiet house being suddenly engulfed in flames. He would pass Britannia Pier, under which the dark and cavernous Uncle Tom's Cabin was housed, and the beach with its shells, donkeys and people, before he arrived at Miss Haddon's School in Albert Square.

Miss Mary Bird Haddon had taken over the school from her father, Revd Thomas Haddon, and sisters. To Charles she was 'kind, cheerful, stout and patient'. His obvious fondness for her school may be explained by his memory of drawing from Vere Foster guides and ballroom dancing – but no lessons. Another great attraction was the dragon-tattooed John Quince, a sergeant in the Norfolk Militia artillery, who drilled

Granny's cabinet.

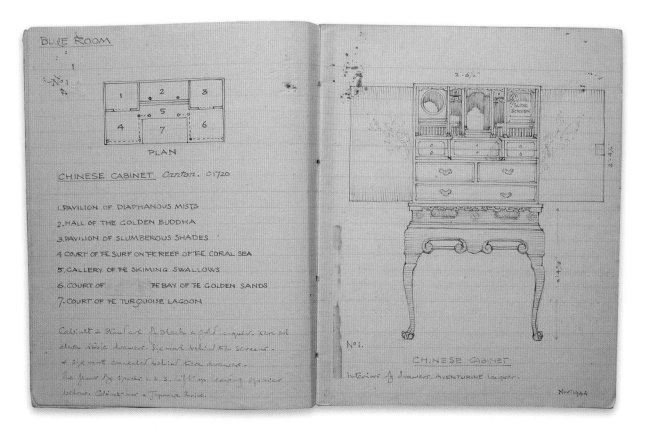

BLUE ROOM

N°1

PLAN

CHINESE CABINET *Canton*. C1720

1.PAVILION OF DIAPHANOUS MISTS
2.HALL OF THE GOLDEN BUDDHA
3.PAVILION OF SLUMBEROUS SHADES
4.COURT OF THE SURF ON THE REEF OF THE CORAL SEA
5.GALLERY OF THE SKIMING SWALLOWS
6.COURT OF   THE BAY OF THE GOLDEN SANDS
7.COURT OF THE TURQUOISE LAGOON

N°1.

CHINESE CABINET

Interiors of drawers. AVENTURINE Lacquer.

Nov 1944

Pages from one of Charles's notebooks.

the children in marching and took them swimming on South Beach. Charles was fascinated by Quince's tattoo, and the mermaid tattoo sported by William, his family gardener at Shortlands, which may in part account for two rooms in Snowshill Manor being named Dragon and Mermaid. Indicative of his future interests, Charles could not remember a single fellow pupil from his days with Miss Haddon, but could recall in great detail the form and contents of the school rooms.

'SCHOOL, THAT DISMAL SPECTRE'

At the age of ten, in 1893, Charles left Great Yarmouth for Eastbourne, where it was intended that he attend St Andrew's School as a boarder. Until a vacancy arose there he attended Timsbury Preparatory School for two terms. Although short in duration it was long enough. He 'disliked it and was extremely bored'. He remembered

the disparity between the sumptuously furnished parts of the school shown to the parents and the 'sordid classrooms … in the dungeons below' not on show. The opposite was true of St Andrew's, which he remembered as having 'an exceptionally happy atmosphere'. Here he became a boarder at Aldro House at the start of the 1894 school year. He struck up a lasting friendship with Revd Edwin Leece Browne who was headmaster of the school; Browne's tenure began with 13 students and ended with over 100. This success may be attributed to his care with the pupils; until a few years before his death he wrote to Charles every year to wish him a happy birthday.

At school Charles 'never had the faintest desire to be top of any classes', his thoughts being 'far away in happier spheres'. He spent his lessons filling the margins of his exercise books with designs for punts or for houses he would build over the pond in the school holidays. Charles's poor opinion of school was much influenced by his intense dislike for boarding, which he regarded as a 'foolish whim' of his parents. Under the dreary daily routines of a school boarder 'the joys of youth just pine away'. After contracting measles on his birthday he conceded that schools were at least useful as a melting pot for 'inescapable childhood epidemics', to avoid having them in adulthood.

ELMSLEY

From late 1893 Paget and Amy had been looking to move out of London. Initially they house-hunted at Fleet, near Farnborough; then at an auction in April 1895 Paget purchased a 'picturesque old fashioned' country house at Yoxford, in Suffolk. It was called Elmsley, although, being built of brick and tile, it had been known as the Red House until 1867. The property comprised 13 acres of land, stables, farm buildings, a walled garden, orchard, tennis court, pond and two cottages. It had a 'pretty but not extensive view of the surrounding countryside'. An obvious attraction to the property for Paget was the station for the main Great Eastern Railway just over a mile away, which gave him an easy connection with London. The Wades redecorated Elmsley and moved in in mid-1896, when Charles was 13.

Charles became extremely fond of Elmsley, which was to remain the family home for 50 years until its eventual sale in 1946. He wrote little directly about Birchwood, the former family home of 13 years, but remembered Yoxford as a 'peaceful and delightful place' with 'old time grace', where his 'childhood sped so happily' by.

Within the house there were three areas of real interest for him. The kitchen 'had more character, more personality, than all the others put together. It always seemed such a happy place … it had an unfailing sense of perfect cheer and comfort, however bleak the day.' The old stairs that led from the first floor to the attics were 'no

ordinary' stairs, as they were 'somewhat erratic', and as such were a 'much more interesting way'. From here Charles and his sisters would clamber 'out onto the leads' to 'Skyland', the rooftop world from which they could look down over Yoxford and across the surrounding countryside. Even in adulthood Charles continued to visit the roof. To this day an inscription on some lead flashing commemorates a rooftop visit by Charles, Connie and family friend Henry Fretz.

Among the house staff were some characters Charles long remembered. To a growing lad the cook, Maria Liley, who was

Top: Elmsley in 1896. From left to right (standing): Connie, Amy, Paget, Olive; (seated): Granny Spencer and Mary Blanche Bulwer. *Above:* Charles with his sister, Olive, on the pond at Elmsley, *c.*1903.

The attic stairs at Elmsley, painted by Charles in 1912.

managed to fit a wife, nine children and 'an immense opinion of his value'. His ego proved his downfall when he was finally dismissed, after telling Paget that 'there cannot be two masters in the place'.

'THE GRAVE OF IMAGINATION'

At the age of 14 Charles left St Andrew's for its 'antithesis': Uppingham School, Rutland. Here as a boarder he was 'imprisoned' in Lorne House, home to 'mournful mysteries, a festering decay'. He recalled the 'foulness of fare', 'evilly cooked meat, tough and underdone with waterlogged vegetables'. 'Cabbage Water Soup' was regularly on the menu, and once it was 'so repulsive' that he and 46 other students refused to eat it so that it was 'sent in cans to the Poor … poor Poor!' He believed that the school motto should have been a variation of Captain Bligh's dictum: 'boys are the lowest form of animal life'.

Finding mathematics, French, Latin and algebra the dreariest of subjects, his dislike for the school was compounded by the athleticism that Dr Selwyn, the headmaster, had determinedly promoted after his appointment in 1888. As remarked in a history of Uppingham: 'The tough, extrovert good games-player found plenty in the school to his taste in Selwyn's time; the sensitive, artistic type by contrast found life hard.' (Christopher) Richard Wynne Nevinson, the well-known First World War artist, wrote:

so proficient in the art of Mrs Beeton, had an obvious appeal. Alfred Emerson was 'the typical old style Coachman, upright with short curling side whiskers. … When on the box seat of the carriage his countenance was immobile. … If he passed his wife when on duty, there was not a slightest flicker of recognition … He would have driven straight on, over her and through her!' Emerson regarded the advent of the motorcar 'with the greatest scorn and would not give way half an inch'.

As a result of this stand-off the Wades were one of the last families in the area to travel by carriage. Eventually progress could not be avoided and Emerson was retired to the garden full-time. In this role he became an 'autocrat' and his employers were visitors in their own garden. Perhaps he was less outspoken than the gardener he replaced – Edward Burnham – whom the Wades had inherited from the previous owner. Burnham lived in one of the small cottages adjoining Elmsley, in which he

[I] was kicked, hounded, caned, flogged, hair-brushed morning noon and night … Games were the order of the day, but I was able to escape grim afternoons chasing the ball by going to the studio to paint and draw, and by accompanying the Art Master Frederick Sydney Robinson in a gig to draw the lovely architecture of Rutland.

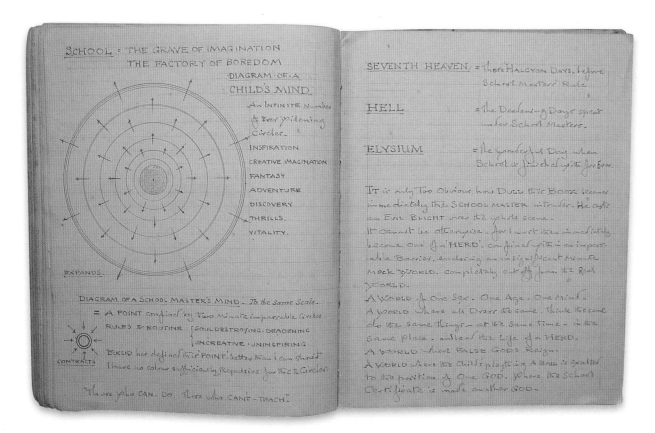

SCHOOL = THE GRAVE OF IMAGINATION
THE FACTORY OF BOREDOM

·DIAGRAM·OF·A·
CHILD'S MIND

An INFINITE Number
of Ever widening
Circles.

INSPIRATION
CREATIVE IMAGINATION
FANTASY
ADVENTURE
DISCOVERY
THRILLS.
VITALITY.

EXPANDS.

DIAGRAM OF A SCHOOL MASTER'S MIND. To the same Scale.
= A POINT confined by Two minute impassable Circles
RULES & ROUTINE { SOUL DESTROYING·DEADENING
                  { UNCREATIVE·UNINSPIRING
CONTRACTS
Euclid has defined this POINT better than I can do it.
I have no colour sufficiently Repulsive for the 2 Circles.

"Those who CAN. DO. Those who CAN'T - TEACH."

SEVENTH HEAVEN = Those HALCYON DAYS before School Masters' Rule.

HELL = The Deadening Days spent under School Masters.

ELYSIUM = the wonderful Day when School is finished quite for Ever.

IT is only Too Obvious how DULL this BOOK became immediately the SCHOOL MASTER intruded. He cast an Evil BLIGHT over the whole scene.
It cannot be otherwise. for I must then immediately become one of a 'HERD'. confined within an impassable Barrier. enclosing an insignificant Minute MOCK WORLD. completely cut off from the Real WORLD.
A WORLD of One Sex. One Age. One Mind.
A WORLD where all Dress the same. Think the same do the same things — at the Same Time — in the Same Place. and lead the Life of a HERD.
A WORLD where FALSE GODS Reign.
A WORLD where the Child's playing a BALL is greater to the position of One GOD. Where the School Certificate is made another GOD.

Charles, who came to Uppingham after Nevinson, similarly escaped the horrors of exercise by frequenting the drawing studio and going with Robinson on sketching tours of the as-yet unspoilt stone villages of Rutland.

Charles wrote expansively about his contempt for schools, calling them 'factories of boredom' and 'graveyards of imagination'. He stated that they were designed for 'destroying all inspiration', 'murdering personality', 'obliterating fantasy', and 'stamping out the standard child'. He believed that a child's mind was unlimited and outward-looking in its search for inspiration, adventure, discovery and creativity, whereas the schoolmaster's mind was confined and inward-looking, bound by rules and routine. He described life as having three phases: Seventh Heaven, 'those halcyon days before school'; Hades, 'those deadening days under school'; and finally, Elysium, 'when school is finished forever'. He concluded: 'I was imprisoned in schools from the age of seven to 19. I have nothing to thank them for. Unmitigated boredom!'

In fact, Charles was only 18 when he left school, and one may feel that this slight exaggeration is consistent with the rest of his rhetoric on the subject. His resentment of school, and romantic self-construction, arguably prevented him from acknowledging the things he took from his schooldays that he might be thankful for. If he formed no enduring friendships with his fellow pupils, his connection to some staff members would last through adulthood, and the art lessons and drawing experience he obtained while there, particularly with Frederick Robinson, were highly influential on his development in the years after leaving school.

Charles Wade's opinion of school depicted in one of his notebooks.

3 Elysium 1901–11

'When at last the dreary deadening days of school were over for ever', Charles entered into training for a profession. His father Paget was employed full-time in the everyday management of the family sugar and cotton business, including the personal estates of his brothers Edwin and Ethelbert. If there were an opportunity to begin an internship in the family business, though, Charles did not take it.

On 17 January 1901 he was indentured as an apprentice architect to Edward Fernley Bisshopp of 32 Museum Street, Ipswich, for a period of four years. It is not known why Bisshopp was chosen, but as the Diocesan Surveyor for Suffolk he would have been

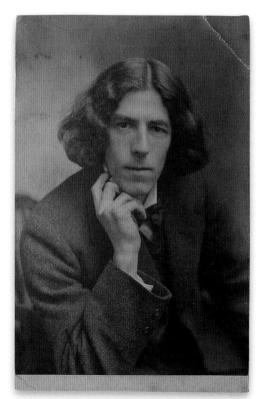

Charles prior to the First World War.

known to the Bulwer family, with its church connections. The conditions of Charles's indenture included that he not 'play at cards or dice tables, or any other unlawful games' which might incur Bisshopp loss or damages. Whilst Charles did not record for posterity his reasons for choosing architecture, looking back on his childhood it was an obvious choice. Architecture had been the backdrop to many of the dramas played out at home and in his imagination, and he took a keen interest in it whilst at school. Charles arrived in Ipswich full of optimism:

> Now at last after all the years of frustration I was free to turn again to all those interests that I had found at Great Yarmouth as a small boy. Ipswich proved an excellent place for this purpose for there was much of architectural interest, both churches and houses of fine timber construction of the sixteenth and seventeenth centuries.

Unfortunately for Charles, Bisshopp was 'not an inspiring architect and he was certainly not an artist'. Charles rather harshly judged his work as unvaried and too formulaic, and that as the Diocesan Surveyor he had swept 'much of the interest out of Suffolk churches'. Bisshopp also had two pastimes which frustrated Charles's professional development. The first was a love of litigation, and Bisshopp spent much time at the offices of Westhorp, Cobbald and Ward, solicitors on the ground floor, challenging clients' protests over his fees. Charles and his colleagues were often employed in painstakingly transcribing Bisshopp's illegible drafts into letters in support of his current case. Bisshopp's other love was fishing. Returning from a fishing trip with crude sketches of his catch, he expected Charles to transform these into 'accurate full size drawings'.

Fortunately, not long after Charles started there were two valuable additions to the office. The atmosphere was lifted with the arrival of a prankster, Edward (Teddy) Alfred Fernley Bisshopp, Bisshopp's son. Even his father was not immune to Teddy's pranks, a memorable one being to replace some of the paint lozenges in Bisshopp's venerable watercolour set (a family heirloom) with replicas made from sealing wax or even liquorice. The apprentices would then hope to catch sight of their master stubbornly endeavouring to draw colour from these impostors. Teddy, who became an actor, was very fond of Charles and they stayed in touch until Teddy's death.

The other addition to the office was certainly a welcome one for Charles's professional development: Henry Munro Cautley, a new partner who would later replace Bisshopp as Diocesan Surveyor. Charles recalled that,

> [Cautley] had sound architectural knowledge and a fine sense of imaginative design. He was always ready to help me with my studies for the RIBA. Cautley had many interesting jobs to carry out and often took me to see the buildings at various stages, which was essential.

Charles boarded in Ipswich with James and Georgiana Walford, their daughter and another boarder. Walford was recommended to Charles by Bisshopp, who had trained his son Henry ten years earlier. Walford had recently begun to take in boarders to support his private but 'scanty' income, which he further supplemented by knitting

socks on a 'little knitting machine' in his study. He sold the socks to 'many a Noble Lord and Viscount' whom he had kept in contact with from a shared past. In his life he had been a commercial traveller and, more recently, a political agent. It is clear from his writings that Charles very much admired this 'exceptionally capable' and 'wonderful old man' and continued to correspond with him until his death in 1915.

Helmets in Dragon.

TREASURE SEEKING

Now with a small but independent income Charles was able to focus determinedly on adding to the craftsmanship collection begun aged seven. Apart from the three French bone shrines bought in 1890, there are no surviving records of Charles's collecting until late October 1900, when he began living in Ipswich, ready to begin his apprenticeship early in the new year. Whilst the purchase of an oak bureau, a pair of walnut chairs dating from 1770 and an applewood chair could be considered of practical use to a young man setting himself up in an independent life, the vast majority of purchases he made now could not. He purchased, among other things, a stuffed flying fox, an 18th-century highwayman's pistol, a portable Buddhist shrine, four odd shoe buckles, two Norwegian headdresses, three samplers, and a set of miniature plaster copies of the Elgin Marbles.

Drawings of Samurai armour from the Green Room in one of Charles's notebooks.

It seems that the scale of Wade's collecting now and in later years was constrained more by his finances – which he did not push to the limit – than by his available exhibition space – which he did. Given that he had only one private room at the Walfords', it is not surprising that Charles was weighed down by items brought back to Elmsley on his weekend visits. For such a large house, his bedroom was surprisingly small. The only photograph of his Elmsley bedroom in existence shows that he had it, understatedly, 'full of quite interesting things' overflowing from Ipswich. It was not just the quantity of items that overwhelmed his rooms but their scale, and they no doubt required space elsewhere in the house and outbuildings at Elmsley. There were the ten square feet of 16th-century oak panelling, the sedan chair he bought in 1903 from outside a second-hand shop in Sedan Street, Ipswich, and the small spinning wheel and

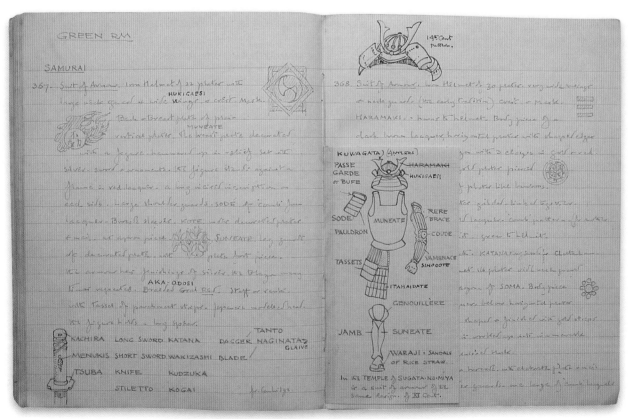

flax wheel. All of these, now at Snowshill Manor, had then to be transported back to Yoxford.

On holiday and weekend visits to Yoxford Charles continued to make purchases. Horace H. Lanham in Framlingham, Suffolk, was well patronised on these home visits. Willoughby Wright, an elderly furniture broker in nearby Dennington, had a 'remarkable accumulation of things' strewn through his house, outbuildings and even garden, where 'furniture, even grandfather clocks, stood out there half hidden by climbing weeds'. Many of the things now in the cottage at Snowshill came from here.

Between 1900 and January 1907, when Charles left Ipswich for London, his records show purchases amounting to £86 6s. Although this may not seem a large sum of money for a serious collector to spend over a six-year period, it should be said that he was just starting out as a collector, supported by only a small income, that many of the items were unfashionable, and that the equivalent sum today would not cover the cost of what he purchased then. Charles recollected of this time that 'I found much that would have been of interest now, but owing to the scarcity of funds I had to be content with a few purchases and the knowledge gained'.

Looking back on his collecting in 1945, in *Days Far Away* Charles stated that he 'intended to keep to English things, but found that there was little with the attraction of colour, save heraldry'. Seeking the richness and drama colour afforded he looked to Spain and Italy, then Persia and eventually to the Far East, where he said 'the three essentials of design, colour and craftsmanship are attained to the fullest'. From the purchases he made during his time in Ipswich it is clear that even then he was not focused on collecting exclusively from England or even the Continent, as he bought a Zulu necklace and a number of Japanese and Chinese items, including in 1903 four

A suit of Samurai armour in the Green Room.

samurai swords and his first suit of samurai armour. This was for many years to remain locked away in a chest because he had nowhere suitable to display it. Long after his death, another suit of samurai armour was found hidden in the window seat in the room called Seraphim at Snowshill Manor.

Charles wrote that he 'received no encouragement from home, being told he was wasting his money on rubbish'. It is clear, though, that his parents did not prevent him from storing much of his ever-growing collection at Elmsley. In fact, contrary to his recollections, his

Above: A model ship in Admiral at Snowshill Manor. *Below:* Charles (centre stage) in the Hampstead Garden Pageant production, 1911.

wider family actively contributed to his collection with Turkish slippers, gold thread and pearls, a tortoiseshell snuffbox, Chinese spectacles and a pair of steel shoe buckles. Granny Spencer gave him knee and shoe buckles and a bone hinged salad spoon and fork. Ethelbert even gifted him two more samurai swords and later two Japanese spears. Further, his family clearly had confidence in his judgement and care, and in the constancy of his interest in craftsmanship and family history.

Before her death in 1904 his great-grandmother Mary Bulwer gifted him family treasures, and her daughter Granny Spencer would bestow on him many heirlooms, including a small chamber organ, a baby dress, and the bands of Augustine Bulwer. His mother gave him a cravat belonging to her father. Others, like the widow of Sam Thurlow, the Yoxford cobbler, also gave him items.

DRAMATIC ART

Another passion that Charles pursued more determinedly was art. Ipswich allowed him the freedom and inspiration to continue to grow as an artist where instruction from Uppingham had left off. As part of his professional portfolio he produced exterior and interior sketches of churches and cathedrals, nearby and further afield. For himself he drew and painted real scenes, like the Neptune Inn, and imaginary ones.

On summer evenings, after the imaginative and physical confines of the office, he would venture down to the harbour to study brigs, schooners, ketches and barges, and analyse them from stem to stern, masthead, rig, tackle and deck fitting. Here on the air 'were the scent of turpentine, tar, hemp oil, maize and grain'. Although the harbourside 'changed from day to day', the one constant was the old hulk *Wolf's Cove*, which lay rotting, 'forlorn, deserted, left astrand at the water's edge',

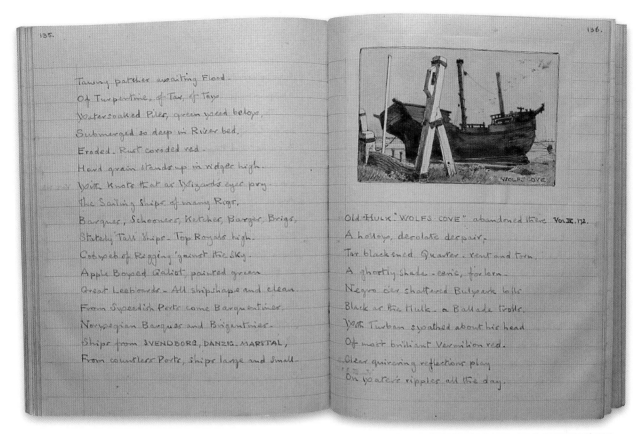

Tawny patches awaiting Flood.
Of Turpentine, of Tar, of Tays
Watersoaked Piles, green weed belays,
Submerged so deep in River bed,
Eroded. Rust corroded red.
Hard grain stands up in ridges high.
With Knots that as Wizard's eyes pry.
The Sailing Ships of many Rigs,
Barques, Schooners, Ketches, Barges, Brigs,
Stately Tall Ships. Top Royals high.
Cobweb of Rigging 'gainst the Sky.
Apple Bowed Galiot, painted green
Great Leeboards. All ship-shape and clean.
From Swedish Ports come Barquentiers.
Norwegian Barques and Brigantines.
Ships from SVENDBORG, DANZIG. MARSTAL,
From countless Ports, ships large and small.

Old Hulk "WOLFS COVE" abandoned there. Vol IX. 172.
A hollow, desolate despair.
Tar blackened Quarter. rent and torn.
A ghostly shade. eerie, forlorn.
Negro oer shattered Bulwark tolls
Black as the Hulk. a Ballade trolls.
With Turban swathed about his head
Of most brilliant Vermilion red.
Clear quivering reflections play
On water's ripples all the day.

until it eventually went to the breaker's yard. Charles wrote of it, painted it and years later would name his model fishing village at Snowshill after it.

Some of his paintings were after works by or in the style of other artists and illustrators: for example, William J. Neatby, a watercolourist and chief designer for Doultons, and the artists Kate Greenaway and Randolph Caldecott, whose illustrations had fired his imagination in childhood. Here again Granny Spencer is found supporting Charles in his efforts as an artist. She gave him Augustine Bulwer's brass drawing instruments and, on his birthday in 1902, Augustine's tempera colours which dated from *c.*1840, signing herself 'affectionate Granny K.B. Spencer'.

Charles found another source of inspiration outside his day job, which totally ignored one of the conditions of his indenture to Bisshopp: not to 'haunt Taverns or Playhouses'. Charles mainly

haunted the Lyceum Theatre in Ipswich, keeping the programmes and collecting reviews of the performances. He went to see the romantic English theatre actor Sir John Martin-Harvey in *After All* in March 1906 and in the theatre programme detailed the individual items of costume worn by the

Top: A poem about the quayside at Ipswich.
Above: Watercolour by Charles of the hulk *Wolf's Cove.*

Charles (left), c.1912, looking increasingly like the actor Martin-Harvey (right).

actors. Here in the audience Charles was enveloped in a heady mix of plot, acting, and the mise en scène of painted backdrops, costume and authentic props which drew him back to previous centuries. Of course, old and archaic buildings, dark interiors and objects had provoked his imagination since early childhood, allowing him to conjure up stories or drawings. He now found that theatre, and especially period drama, could be an intensely provocative medium.

The historical costume and staging he saw in theatrical productions inspired his collecting and the development of his own more dramatic personal image. Charles had promotional postcards of the great actors and actresses of the age posing in period costume. He particularly focused on Sir Henry Irving, the famous Victorian actor, and Martin-Harvey, who bought Irving's collection of genuine historical props when he died suddenly in 1905. Taking their lead Charles began having portrait photographs of himself taken in historic dress, often against period backdrops from his own ever-increasing collection. It is hard to miss

Charles's similarity to Martin-Harvey in his own photographs, in which – over time – he modelled his hairstyle on the long hair worn by the actor in this period. Many years later Edwin Lutyens would compare the elderly Charles's face to 'a death mask of Henry Irving'.

Charles bought a number of historical costumes belonging to various well-known painters. In 1907 he purchased a coat and waistcoats which had once belonged to Sir Henry Raeburn. He obtained military costume from other collectors including a livery coat with the royal monogram from Lawrence Alma-Tadema. Through theatre Charles found his purpose and became a director, provocateur and conjurer. He was not collecting items of costume and craftsmanship in isolation, but with the aim of creating a wider historical backdrop.

ARTISTIC VALUES

In London in early June 1904, Charles qualified for RIBA studentship. Whilst in

Bisshopp's office Charles produced, with the assistance of Cautley, a full 'Design for a country house in Suffolk', which appears never to have been executed. Charles's only known professional output for the practice was alterations to 'The Grove', in Cumberland Street at Woodbridge in 1906 for a Mr Beeton. It is probable that he left Ipswich and Bisshopp's practice just after he was elected an associate of RIBA in March 1907.

CHARLES PAGET WADE. ÆT. 27.

Before securing a new position, however, he embarked for the Continent. During his first trip to Europe Charles visited Venice and Verona. He painted, and collected, among other things, a pair of brass lamps, satin waistcoats and a copper cow bell. He returned to England and Yoxford in late May and began working industriously on a number of architectural schemes. Between 2 October and 25 November he spent 236 hours designing and completing his final plans for a fictitious building named Almesbury Court. At this time the floorplans and elevations for many of his designs included poems which related to the spaces shown. In recognition of his qualification as an architect, that year Charles had his portrait painted by the influential Australian landscape artist Tom Roberts. This portrait still hangs at Snowshill Manor.

In the year 1907 Charles also completed his unpublished manuscript *Country Cottage and Its Garden*. Full of pen-and-ink drawings, poems and quotes, it is structured as a tour of a fictitious cottage located in the county of Rutland, which he had fallen in love with as a student. Setting off from the white wooden front gate, the reader is led not just through a cottage and garden but also through the architectural and craft values Charles would hold dear throughout his life. The worth of vernacular architecture and design born of carefully selected materials and character, wrought by the skill of craftsmen and their

hand tools, is celebrated in these pages.

Here, in his clearest endorsement of the values of the Arts and Crafts movement, the effect of writings by Mackay Hugh Baillie Scott and John Ruskin is strongly felt. His bibliography records other influences, including Sir Edwin Lutyens and Gertrude Jekyll, and historical studies on vernacular architecture in the counties and various crafts such as leadwork and glazing. He champions the role of the craftsman, the use of the adze, chisel and plane over the 'remorseless circular saw', and the importance of allowing the

Top: Charles in 1910, painted by Thomas Roberts.
Above: Charles's RIBA certificate, 1907.

A watercolour
by Charles of his
design for the
'Great Wall' at
Hampstead Garden
Suburb, 1908.

natural qualities of materials to win over superficial decoration. He demonstrates the significance of colour and natural and artificial light. Furniture should harmonise with the house and space. There is a place for mottoes and poetry, but none for the 'tyranny' of ornaments and miniatures.

We see for the first time the values realised in the physical works later undertaken at Snowshill Manor and also the essential relationship between house and garden that would be consummated 15 years later in the design of Snowshill Manor garden. At the same time Charles entered a competition in *The Studio* (an illustrated magazine for fine applied art) with a design for a small garden entitled 'Peaceful hours', winning two guineas as second prize.

DESIGNING A CAREER
Since returning from the Continent Charles had been searching for a position

at a suitable architectural practice in London, without success. A letter he received in November from the architect William Flockhart suggests he was soon to be working for him. Flockhart's reputation for creativity would seem to make him an ideal employer for Charles. However, he later warns Charles not to make any arrangements to this end, as he apparently has had second thoughts and appoints Oliver Hill instead; Hill would become a close friend of Charles many years later. Flockhart nonetheless wrote, perhaps of the Almesbury Court designs:

I cannot possibly express the delight I have had looking over your drawings. I think your work is most wonderful and shows a delightful architectural imagination; I wonder you do not put them together in book-form – I am sure they would be appreciated.

Instead Charles was appointed as architectural assistant to Raymond Unwin in February 1908. Unwin was an engineer, 'architect, planner and visionary' greatly influenced by the writings of Ruskin and William Morris. Having completed the Letchworth Garden City development, he and his cousin and business partner, architect Barry Parker, were appointed as architect and surveyor to design the Hampstead Garden Suburb, then in its first phase. Unwin designed it to be picturesque and without uniformity, and avoided any individual house's outlook being encroached upon by a neighbouring house. Many independent architects were commissioned to design houses for the Suburb, and Charles's involvement in the project personally acquainted him with some of the foremost British architects of the time, including Lutyens and Baillie Scott.

Unwin's side of the partnership was based at his home at Wyldes Farm in Hampstead. With up to 40 staff working in it, the office was 'convivial' and placed great store on the value of traditional and vernacular architecture. With this appointment Charles began to express himself more freely, both professionally and privately. He became lifelong friends with a number of the staff and independent architects, including Guy Dawber, Charles H.B. Quennell, Arthur J. Penty, (Thomas) Alwyn Lloyd, (Henry) Clifford Hollis, (Alfred) Hugh Mottram and Herbert Welch. Welch accompanied Charles on many painting trips into the countryside.

Charles was to make a significant contribution to the artistic output of the practice. It is unclear whether all of the Hampstead Garden buildings attributed to him were solely of his design or whether he worked up and gave artifice to Unwin's basic concepts. One important feature Unwin had Charles design in 1908 was the 'Great Wall', which formed the boundary

between the Garden Suburb and the Hampstead Heath extension beyond. Constructed from brawn brick, with twitten arches and gazebos and gateways, the wall and the spirit of the Suburb were inspired by the architecture and character of the medieval walled town of Rothenburg which had captivated Unwin. At this time Charles had not visited it, but was influenced by Unwin, and thus by the architecture and layout of such ancient north European towns.

Charles was valued for his artistic skill, but also for his ability to create interest and drama in his architectural detailing. He designed distinctive hooded balconies for cottages in Asmuns Place, Nos 1 and 3, and the large, arched entry twittens

Charles (centre) with his colleagues from Raymond Unwin's office, Clifford Hollis and Hugh Mottram, 1909.

An imaginary church cloisters, painted by Charles when in Dominica en route to St Kitts, 1910.

for the terraced cottages further along. In 1909 he was tasked with the design of No. 3 Rotherwick Road. Along with No. 1, which was given to Hollis, it formed the gateway into the new suburb from Golders Green, and was therefore critical to Unwin's overall scheme. Charles provided detailing for the Club House (Folk Hall), Willifield Green, which was intended to be at the centre of Suburb society, but this unfortunately was demolished after damage by a land mine in 1940. The Orchard, built 1909–10, another Parker and Unwin design detailed by Charles, was demolished in 1970.

Every night after work, Charles would return to his 'upper chamber' in Fortune Hill where he continued to design. This was to remain his London address until after the First World War and his permanent move to Snowshill Manor in 1920. Here his nocturnal industry varied. On St Valentine's Day 1908 he designed an elaborate, gilded, griffon weather vane on a wooden octagonal pillar. The following year he produced a complete plan (unexecuted) for a Folk Hall 'for minstrels, Morris dances and peasant plays'. He also designed a sampler depicting a cottage in a style he would have used for Hampstead.

His most ambitious private and fanciful architectural scheme was his plans for the fictitious abbey and convent of St Frances of Assisi in a vale by 'Alconbury'. He annotated the principal site plan: 'Charles Wade did the drawings for the Abbey in 14 weeks between Feb to May c.1908 in his 26th year in Hampstead. May the next be better.' The plan used gilt paint with mother-of-pearl set into the backing paper to denote water features. This was a common detail on his site plans; some even had woven ribbon borders. The plan, impressive as it was, formed only a part of the artistic output which 'Alconbury Abbey' provoked in Charles. He produced a large number of representations of the interior and exterior of the walled religious community, executed in watercolour, pen and ink, and gouache. In these he used a turquoise colour that was to figure consistently in his future designs and would finally materialise at Snowshill Manor on interior and exterior joinery; it is now known as Wade Blue.

This period is noteworthy not only for the skill and attraction of Charles's architectural designs, but for the large number of associated pen-and-ink sketches and watercolours that he produced. These increasingly brought him to the attention of his friends and colleagues. He was not merely an able artist; his style and imaginative renderings made him sought-after. Unwin had recognised his ability early on and was so impressed that he tasked him with producing illustrations for his forthcoming book, *Town Planning Practice* (1909). Charles produced over 30 pen-and-ink illustrations for this seminal text, including a drawing of the cottage he had designed at No. 1 Rotherwick Road. Some drawings depicted imaginary streetscapes to help illustrate Unwin's theories. Others portrayed real streets in English and European towns, though it is unclear whether Charles actually travelled to the Continent or relied on photographs. Twelve of his illustrations were also included in *Town Planning & Modern Architecture at the Hampstead Garden Suburb* (1909).

Charles also provided illustrations to accompany his friend Michael Bunney's proposal for Gidea Park housing development and William Henry Ward's scheme for the Cutteslowe Garden Village outside Oxford.

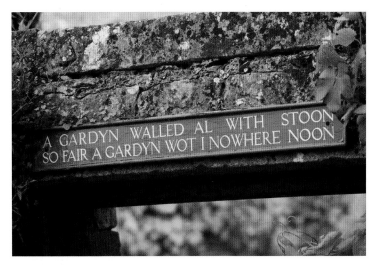

Above: Inscription in the garden at Snowshill Manor. *Left:* The letter box at the front door of Snowshill Manor featuring the coat of arms that Charles created for himself.

THOSE 'EMERALD ISLES'

Between February and May 1910 Charles accompanied his parents on perhaps his first trip to the West Indies, principally St Kitts. By this time there had been a change in the make-up of the family business. His two remaining uncles, Ethelbert and Edwin, had died within a week of each other in 1908. Edwin, who had remained unmarried and was bankrupt, died at his lodgings in Brixton, London. Aged only 52, his death

certificate attributed the cause to 'general paralysis, convulsions and exhaustion', descriptors for neurosyphilis, a tertiary form of the syphilis he must have contracted years before.

Ethelbert, who had been unwell for many months with cirrhosis of the liver, died of heart failure in London four days after his younger brother. Ethelbert had married a German woman, Mathilde Seeler, in the months before his death, though they had pretended to be married in the 1901 census when living together. They were childless.

By the time of Ethelbert and Edwin's deaths, Paget had become increasingly involved with managing his private estates and diversifying the wider family business. He was the first to plant cotton commercially on the islands of St Kitts and Montserrat from 1902. No doubt the expectation would have been that Charles would now become more involved in supporting Paget in his endeavours. The sugar industry was also being revolutionised at this time, with the conversion of sugar cane centralised to the Basseterre Sugar Factory constructed in 1911. Construction of a railway was also underway to link the factory and sugar estates. Due to their location, the Wade estates were some of the first to benefit from the rail link.

NO FEE, NO INTERFERENCE

Back in London, from May to July 1911, Charles exhibited at the House and Home Exhibition at the Whitechapel Art Gallery. Organised by Henrietta Barnett of the Hampstead Garden Trust, with Seymour Lucas, Baillie Scott and Lutyens, the exhibition promoted 'an intelligent interest in the material surrounding of our lives' and in how 'traditional art that had made nearly every corner of English towns and villages full of beauty … gave way to violent negation of all beauty that we now see at every turn in our streets'. Unwin was also involved in the exhibition and a number of juniors from his office were exhibitors. Charles displayed some paintings there, plus a model he had conceived and built between 1902 and 1904 whilst articled to Bisshopp at Ipswich. This was a model of a fictitious 18th-century Red Lion Inn, complete with barrels, outside benches and a tavern sign on a post. It was supplemented with colourful floorplans and a written description.

Charles's activity at Hampstead and 'Alconbury', and with a model village he had begun to design and build, reveals his love of community life as well as craftsmanship. Yet whilst he shared many of the ideals of the Arts and Crafts movement, he was no socialist. He, like his immediate family, was a conservative by nature and never politically active. He did not share his mother's and sisters' inclination to use their wealth and free time to make donations and do good deeds for the less fortunate,

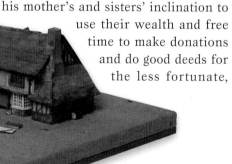

Charles's model of the Red Lion Inn.

though he followed his parents' example in showing benevolence to his employees and appreciating his close friends.

His wealth allowed him the time and means to be a craftsman and an artist. However, whilst he celebrated the skill of other craftsmen and, to a limited degree, became a patron, he did so for personal reasons and did not actively champion their resurrection politically as John Ruskin and William Morris had done years earlier. Instead he expended much of his wealth in collecting examples of their work which appealed to him aesthetically, imaginatively and intellectually. He was nostalgic for the world in which these objects were created and the human condition that was manifest in them. He mourned this world's passing and was resigned to its loss. He memorialised the craftsmen in their creations which he collected.

The House and Home Exhibition was to be Charles's farewell to his position as an assistant to Unwin and an architect, though he remained registered until his death 45 years later. As congenial as the Hampstead Garden project was, someone of Charles's creativity and nonconformist disposition would necessarily feel the architect-client relationship to be characterised by constraint and compromise. In a pen-and-ink depiction of the grave garth of his fictional Alconbury Abbey is a headstone on which can be read the following epitaph: 'Here Lyeth one Charles Wade an architect little known.'

Charles was selfish, insofar as he had a single-minded determination to create on his own terms. A close friend later explained that Charles stopped practising as an architect because he was scornful of many of his clients' tastes and concluded, 'no fee, no interference' with his own. Charles instead turned to art, and in particular painting and illustrating. With the prospect of greater freedom, he left the employment of Raymond Unwin in June 1911.

A watercolour of the burial ground of Alconbury Abbey, painted by Charles in 1908. His own headstone is shown.

Art and Devastation 1911–19

As appreciation of Charles's artistic abilities grew beyond his circle of architect friends, he was introduced to other artists, like the portrait painter Henry (Harry) Harris Brown, and Sir George Clausen RA, the notable landscape painter and official war artist. This attention encouraged him to pursue a career in art, and he soon received commissions to illustrate two books.

Elizabeth (Betty) Murray next to the model village of Fladbury (later Wolf's Cove), laid out at Charles's lodging in Hampstead, *c*.1910.

The first came from Kate Murray (*née* Warren) to illustrate her novel *The Spirit of the House*. Between 1911 and 1913 he provided 38 watercolour plates and pen-and-ink drawings, one set of floorplans, and a map of the novel's wider landscape. There were three central characters: Oliver Caldicott, Fiammetta Tapper and Caldicott Court, an ancestral home and its garden. The vernacular architecture of Rutland can be clearly recognised; the outward appearance of Caldicott Court was inspired by Charles's visit to Rockingham Castle as a schoolboy. In Caldicott Court and gardens we see also a premonition of Snowshill Manor and its collection. Here, as at Snowshill, 'there is no breath of the modern spirit, no hint of the restlessness, the noise, the turmoil of this age'.

Charles's influence perhaps ran deeper than the illustrations, helping the author flesh out the backdrop to the narrative and the character and appearance of Oliver, whose 'life [was] spent among beautiful possessions'. *The Times Literary Supplement* commented:

> … one even had a fear that the author shared Oliver's preference for past things over present human beings; a fear fostered by the careful descriptions of 'Caldicott Court: an imaginary house', its gardens and surroundings … Of Mr Wade's drawings we have only one criticism. Why has Caldicott Court scarcely a window?

How Charles first met Kate, a lecturer in literature at a London girls' college, is unknown, but their acquaintance may have resulted from their shared love for the theatre. Charles acted as 'general aesthetic adviser' for her Christmas play performed at the Hampstead Garden Institute in 1911, and played the part of Lord Herbert. A lasting and valued friendship was struck with her, her husband Donald and their only child, Elizabeth (Betty) Kate Murray. Charles later produced a further six illustrations for Kate's sequel to *The Spirit of the House*, 'Fiammetta's Return', published in the 23 November 1925 issue of *The Sphere*.

The strength of his friendship with Kate provoked one of his more extraordinary creations, for young Betty. Since childhood he had been fascinated by models as tangible

backdrops to the stories and adventures of his imagination. Now, to capture Betty's own imagination, he created a fanciful village called Fladbury which he laid out in the garden at his residence, No. 9 Temple Fortune Hill. He worked through the evenings planning and constructing cottages, an inn, a railway station, a canal complete with locks, and even a visiting fair. The village – now in a different guise – and the Red Lion Inn are now at Snowshill Manor.

This project competed with an even more challenging commission in 1911, to capture the personality of Bruges in pen and ink for Mary Josephine Stratton's *Bruges: A Record and an Impression*, to be published by Harry Batsford. Stratton wrote that 'Mr Wade's drawings and my own enjoyment of the work are my excuses for yielding to the temptation to write this book'.

Charles set off to Bruges and began his exhausting programme of outdoor sketching to produce 113 images of venerable architecture and cityscape. The book was published in 1914, a poignant moment as the German Army had just invaded Belgium and occupied the city. *The Daily Telegraph*, like other reviewers, complimented the illustrations, saying, 'Mr Wade's exquisite drawings are so true to the inspiration of the place that everyone who has known and loved Bruges can read into them the sentiment which the place first imbued into him.' Years later Batsford published Jasper Salwey's *Sketching in Lead Pencil for Architects and Others* (1926), which holds up Charles's sketches of Bruges as fine examples.

A DEATH IN PARADISE

In November 1911 Charles's father left for his annual visit to St Kitts, this time without his wife but with Connie. On the day he left, Paget gave a last gift to his son: two shirts belonging to Solomon Wade. In

An ink drawing of Bruges that Charles produced for Mary Stratton's *Bruges: A Record and an Impression*, published in 1914.

early December Paget, who suffered from a long-term throat complaint, caught a bad chill. After ten days he improved, but his condition suddenly deteriorated again and he returned to bed. By Christmas Eve the Wades' St Kitts doctor, Dr Fretz, felt compelled to write to Charles from Paget's White House bedside that 'there is little chance of recovery' and to 'be brave and bear it through and be a comfort to Mrs Spencer and Olive'. On receiving the news of

Paget Augustus Wade, Charles Wade's father.

The Golden Hour, painted by Charles in Dominica in 1913.

'universally respected', and his death was seen as a great loss to the West Indies. Amy wrote to Charles stating that they must emulate Paget's 'sense of honour in all his dealings' and his great consideration for his employees. Granny Spencer, Paget's mother-in-law, and his mother and sisters had relied on him as a 'trusted advisor' and manager of the family business; up until this time, so had Charles. This changed after his father's death as he was drawn into the business with the guidance of his mother.

Amy wrote from St Kitts warning her son that she and he would be taking on great responsibilities. Amy was so determined to gain sole control of all the family sugar and cotton interests in St Kitts and Montserrat that she paid an overly generous price to buy out Paget's sisters Susan and Fanny, and his widowed sister-in-law Mathilde. Living in London Charles was now frequently charged by Amy to be the go-between for the day-to-day family business duties and for Sendall and Wade. However, she remained very much in control and her frequent letters, whilst touched with maternal affection, were often dominated by business updates, appointments and financial transactions. She left him in no doubt when she was addressing him as an

her husband's grave condition, Amy left for St Kitts on 20 December. She arrived only in time to console and care for her daughter Connie, whom shock had made very ill. Paget had died on Christmas Day, aged 62, of cardiac failure due to influenza. As was then the practice, the death certificate registered him as 'coloured'.

Paget, an innovator, energetic employer and generous benefactor had been

employee and when he was 'careless' and fell short of meeting her expectations.

Charles found it difficult to talk to others about Paget's death, initially channelling his energy into designing his father's gravestone at Christ Church, St Kitts. Of all the children, though, it was the highly strung younger daughter Olive, who had remained at home in England with her mother, who was to suffer the most from this event. In early 1912 she had a nervous breakdown and was admitted to the Bethel Hospital in Norwich. She was briefly discharged in October, but her father's death continued to weigh heavily on her and she was rehospitalised the following year. There, under the delusion that she had made a vow of fasting and silence, she spent a fortnight refusing to eat, drink or speak.

Amy found her daughter's letters, filled with accounts of visions, distressing and a sign of serious deterioration. The doctors disagreed and assured her that this should be considered progress and an improvement on apathy. Olive indeed improved and was duly released for a final time in August 1914, but she never fully recovered. Rightly or wrongly, henceforth she was treated with great care as one would a sweet but naive child. She was frequently sent to stay with members of her extended family and was never given any real independence. To those on the periphery it appeared that she was treated as second best and intellectually inferior. She was not unintelligent, though, and had a great knowledge of wildlife and was, like Charles, quite an authority on heraldry. Although it has been said that Amy resented having stayed in England with Olive when Paget was dying, she devoted much care to her and any resentment may be a misreading of the frustration and worry that Olive continued to cause her mother and her family.

The friendship of the Murrays, which now extended to Charles's mother and

sisters, was a great comfort. Betty, aged nine, visited the Wades on her own in August 1912, and Charles came up from London to stay at Elmsley especially. During this visit, his friend Don, Kate Murray's husband, wrote to Charles telling him how their daughter Betty's dog, Toby, having covered himself not in glory but something altogether less savoury, had made his way into the next-door neighbour's house and made 'an awful mess' there. Toby, no longer welcome, was no more. As proof of Don's trust in Charles's care of Betty, he asked him to break the news to her and avoid creating any hope for another dog in the near future. He thoughtfully enclosed a note for Charles to read out if he were lost for words.

Pool, or *Silent Pool*, painted by Charles from the SS *Tagus* en route to St Kitts, 1913.

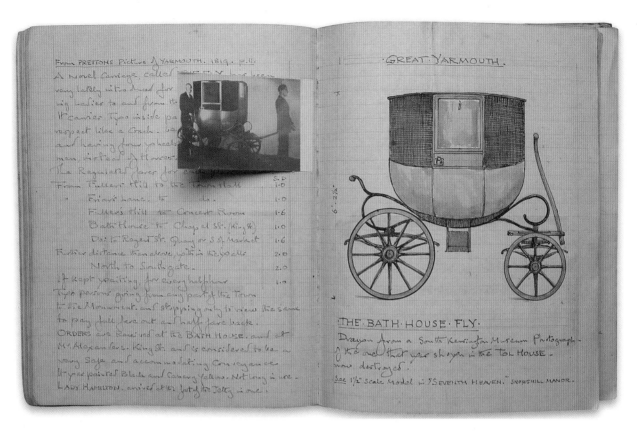

The Bath House Fly.
Great Yarmouth.

Pages from one of Charles Wade's notebooks.

Charles returned to St Kitts with Amy and Connie in February 1913 to become more acquainted with Mansion Estate, which he had inherited and was being managed for him, and the wider family business interests. With a growing profile in the industry his taste in fashion came under scrutiny from Amy, who complained to Charles about the 'ridiculous suit' he was intending to travel to St Kitts in. Travelling independently of his mother and sister he stopped off in Dominica and took the opportunity to paint and draw. In St Kitts he managed to fit this around his business and professional commitments, while also helping out the Revd Jullion by specifying the repairs to St Mary's Church in Cayon, where he had succeeded Paget as a generous subscriber. Charles returned to England in late May.

A COLLISION OF CARRIAGES

In spite of his St Kitts commitments, Charles's collecting continued unabated. In fact, the family business and his private estate allowed him to collect items of higher value and scale and with more frequency. In June 1913 he bought an oak bed from Phillips of Hitchin, Hertfordshire, writing proudly to his friends about it. That year he also bought the Dearing family 'State chariot' (*c*.1790), a yellow travelling coach

that once belonged to the Brandreth family, and a coach that had belonged to Countess Cowper, later the wife of Prime Minister Palmerston. These all came from coach builder Ralph E. Sanders of Hitchin. The coaches were stored at Yoxford, where Charles spent his visit in March 1914 getting very dirty cleaning and restoring them.

Moving from horse to manpower Charles stopped in Norwich in June and bought his first sedan chair. In December he purchased a carved and painted chariot from a London dealer. This chariot can still be seen in the garden of Snowshill Manor. Sanders had not seen the last of Charles, and in May 1915 he returned to buy two more carriages and a sleigh. One of these, a travelling coach, once belonged to the family of the poet Algernon Swinburne. With all of these coaches his friend Motty asked Charles with amusement, 'Are you going to parade through the country in them?' Charles did not.

This assortment of transportation and furniture bought in and around Suffolk put extreme pressure on the storage space available to Charles at Yoxford. Amy cautioned him against overfilling his rooms, but remained interested and supportive. She attended an auction on his behalf and reported back that he had failed to win the globe or the Charles I needlework that he wanted. Having been kept informed of his purchases, Revd Jullion wrote to him presciently, saying, 'You'll soon need a whole house to yourself, not just rooms'.

COSTUME AND CREATIVITY

Charles's interest in historic costume persisted. Clara Millard of Teddington, Middlesex, proved a rich source of interesting and provocative items. Here in 1912 Charles bought two helmets for £1 10s (an average week's wage was about £1 4s at this time). He also bought a side drum (£4 4s) and a pair of postillion boots once

owned by Maria Theresa of Austria (£10). The side drum had been bought on the understanding that it had been used by the Coldstream Guards at Waterloo. In London the threshold of an antiques shop in St John's Wood, owned by Mrs Mina Solomon, was crossed at great cost. Between Charles's earliest recorded visit to the shop in August 1910 and his last in October 1915 he made 39 visits, purchasing 179 items of historic costume at a cost of around £306 – nearly four times the average annual wage in 1915.

Charles's costume collection was drawing attention. When Edgar Bundy, the successful painter of historical subjects, needed a costume for his daughter, 'ten

One of the oldest sedan chairs in the United Kingdom, located in Meridian.

Above, left and right: Charles dressed in 17th-century costume from his own collection, *c.*1910.
Right: Charles at the time he began working at Parker and Unwin in 1908.

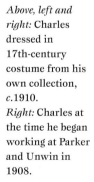

years old but fairly big', to wear to the botanical gardens, he asked Charles. In 1912 Charles hosted a 'Ladies' Party' to show off his collection. Tony Sarg, an Anglo-German puppeteer and illustrator, invited Charles to a New Year's Eve party and asked that he wear one of his 'fascinating costumes'. Sarg sketched Wade smoking a pipe, wearing a dressing gown, and facing a table with books and a human skull.

Charles continued to work on his own career as an artist, and to this end he received tuition from May Butler George, an Australian artist specialising in miniatures. Charles, along with Betty, who often accompanied him on visits to friends and acquaintances, sat for miniature portraits by George. Charles's portrait was exhibited at the Paris Autumn Salon in 1912.

George invited Charles to join a new sketch club, which included mixed portrait sitting with professional models and whose members included Mary Stratton. She believed that it would be good for him, 'giving him loose line and broader treatment'. Her judgement was that, 'You are really great in many ways, if only you could get lost, you would be a great artist. Your work is too "tight", too well ordered – you have the necessary poetic feeling and a very great imagination.'

Through 1914 Charles was again engaged in producing a large number of watercolours for Kate Murray, this time for a children's story called *The Strange Adventures of Nemo and Nulla*. A typed draft of the story was completed in December 1913 and was dedicated by Kate, the author, and Charles, the artist, to Betty. Betty was the inspiration for the story of two dolls that inhabit a castle. These watercolour illustrations are of a far higher quality and more imaginative in subject than those he produced for *The Spirit of the House*. Amy noted, 'you have been very industrious with your paint brush lately'. Ever the businesswoman, she was concerned that it 'was a book that not many publishers would truck', since 'People who would like the pictures would consider it burdened by the text'. Interest in the book proposal did not improve and Charles's friend Motty wrote to him saying, 'sorry your books have not a better show'. He suggested: 'You know with your taste for good things you ought to write a book and illustrate it … I always feel as if you are just wasting yourself. Pardon the plain speaking.'

The Strange Adventures of Nemo and Nulla was never published, although the manuscript and illustrations survive at Snowshill.

Charles saw a lot of the Murrays and in Betty, like her mother, he found imagination and creativity which he actively encouraged. Betty was a kindred spirit and provided him with justification for creating imaginary worlds. Her correspondence to Charles was invariably full of news about the fictitious Lord Mex and his family, whose world Charles had assisted Betty in creating. A few

Dr Pedanteus (above) and *The Shoebill and the Penguin play patience* (left), painted by Charles for *The Strange Adventures of Nemo and Nulla*.

years before the war Charles had made Betty a doll's house for Lord Mex and his family to live in, which now stands amongst the collection at Snowshill Manor. She in turn designed clothes for the dolls.

By 1915, when Betty was 12, poetry had become increasingly dominant. Charles had acted as her amanuensis since she was eight, writing her poems down in notebooks that remain in his archives. On the inside cover of one Charles wrote, 'Elizabeth Kate Murray – my favourite author born Feb 1902'. In early October 1915 he sent a manuscript copy of her poems to be typed up for binding, before giving it to her maternal grandparents.

In December 1914 Charles completed what he described as a mechanised front door bell. It was in the form of a black-painted rectangular cabinet, small enough to be mounted on the wall. The front of

Nemo and Nulla follow the Pied Piper to the shore (opposite), *Nemo and Nulla and the Pirate Ship* (above) and *Nemo and Nulla discover story book land* (left), painted by Charles for *The Strange Adventures of Nemo and Nulla.*

Large doll's house in Mermaid including Robert Taylor's grocer's shop. The house dates from c.1800.

the cabinet had a large opening through which a stage depicting a north European marketplace could be seen. The mechanism was powered by the door through which the visitor passed, opening and closing. The power generated set in motion figures which, to music, exited one of the buildings and moved across the market square, disappearing from view into another building. On the front of the cabinet below the stage opening is a poem that Charles painted on well after its completion, as it ends with the words, 'Charles Wade made me December 1914. Being the first year of the Great war.' This mechanised model shows his desire to create a more interactive and provocative environment in which items are more than they first seem.

A CALL TO ARMS
Charles's collecting to date shows that he was drawn to weapons, armour and especially military uniforms because of their colour, regalia and dramatic possibilities. In May 1914, aged 31, he bought £150 worth

of costume, including military hats and coats, from Fenton and Sons of New Oxford Street, London. However, when Britain declared war on Germany in August that year, Charles's fascination with military accoutrements apparently did not translate to patriotic fervour.

Eight days into the war Amy wrote to Charles asking whether he thought it was splendid that so many young men were volunteering. She also asked him what he was doing for the country in need, because she and his sisters were doing all they could. She had sent Paget's saddles to the army, along with his field glasses. Whenever Charles returned to Elmsley he

Left: Another doll's house in Mermaid. *Above:* A watercolour by Betty Murray of her bedroom, showing the doll's house that Charles made for her. *Below:* The mechanised door bell created by Charles.

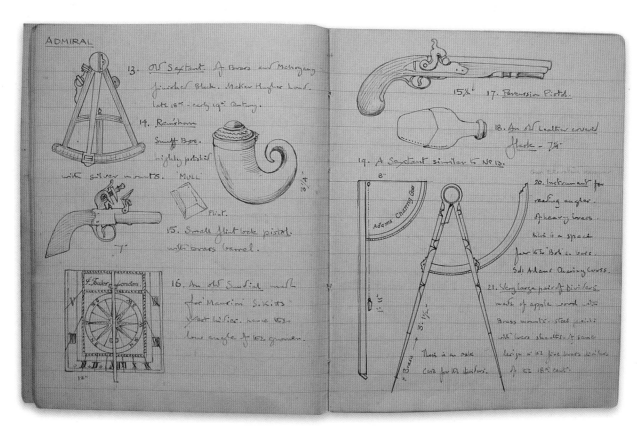

Charles produced handwritten room inventories for the collection at Snowshill Manor. These pages are for Admiral.

found his mother and two sisters engaged in hospital work and knitting scarves. Here he would receive a list of odd carpentry jobs to complete, such as lifting his mother's bedroom floor to correct a shake, or replacing a latch. Whilst he was active in supporting his family on their 'home front', there is no evidence that he was actively engaged in any work for the war effort.

Until now Charles's exposure to the war had been limited. His collecting had tailed off from his feverish pre-war activity – in large part due to the wartime interruption of his income from St Kitts – and he had not been directly affected by the physical horrors of war. He was not unaware of them, of course. Twenty-nine men from Yoxford, 181 in Golders Green and Hampstead Garden Suburb, and many from his schools were killed. In 1915 a family friend, Geoff Scrimgeour, was shot in the arm from a ricochet off a fellow soldier's cap badge. There is no first-hand documentary

evidence from this period to reveal Charles's attitude to the war, and subsequently he never recounted his wartime experiences. What is clear is that he did not volunteer for active service. The reasons for this can be seen in his life leading up to this point. He was a nonconformist and the regimented and athletic life of the army, like that of boarding school, was at odds with his nature. Since leaving school, aside from family and business, Charles had determinedly pursued his own interests in collecting, architecture and art.

It might appear that he was unconcerned about joining up, but a letter from Olive in late November 1915 attests to his active efforts to avoid military service through an exemption, by attempting to gain employment in an aircraft factory – a protected industry. The Military Service Act of 27 January 1916 brought conscription into play for the first time in the war, and any chance that Charles had for passively

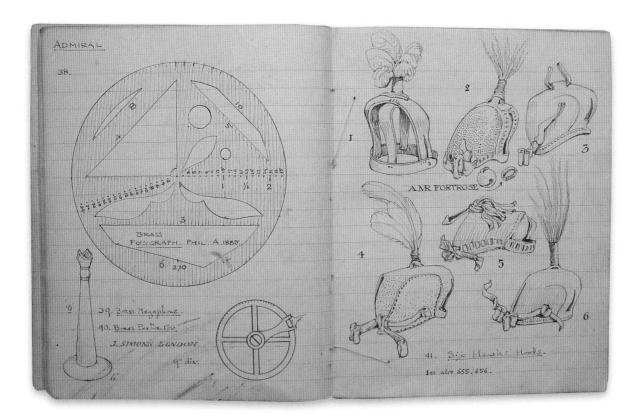

escaping military service was gone. Don Murray, now a major serving on the Western Front, wrote to encourage Charles to get a commission in the engineers or artillery. Murray told Charles, 'I of course quite understand why you have not joined up but ordinary people don't and whilst I think you would find the ranks pretty stiff I am sure you would be able to … fit in as an officer.' In early February, in response to a letter from the military, Charles enlisted at the Bedford Recruiting Office.

He had not yet lost all hope of evading active service, however. Later that month Olive wrote that the family were anxious about the result of his appeal to the Military Service Tribunal and wondered whether the date had been fixed for the hearing yet. It seems Charles was a 'non-conscientious applicant' to the Military Service Tribunal, as there is no evidence that he had a health issue or a moral objection, and certainly he could not call upon a religious one.

Instead, he pursued an exemption on the grounds of occupation.

He was not alone. By July 1916, 748,587 men called up had appealed to a Military Service Tribunal. By the end of the war, just over a third of the army was made up of conscripted men. Charles's earlier efforts to get employment in an aircraft factory had failed, so his enlistment form was the last throw of the dice. It records his occupation as 'sugar planter', rather than architect or artist. No record survives of the hearing – records were destroyed by the Ministry of Health in 1921 – but it is clear that his case failed and he accepted his fate as an active participant in the war. In May 1916 in Bedford he had a medical examination, and being deemed to be in good health was approved for general service in the field. Due to his skills, he was chosen for service in the Royal Engineers. The following month he took a last trip to Rutland to stay with Robinson, his former school art

No. 2 Reinforcement Company of the East Anglia Division Royal Engineers. He was initially stationed at a Royal Engineer No. 4 Base Depot at Rouen, France. He was then sent on to join the East Anglia 483rd Field Company attached to the Third Army of the British Expeditionary Force.

If he did keep a contemporary written record of his service, it did not survive. Later in life whilst he wrote of his childhood, life in Ipswich, London and later, he chose not to recount this period with any great determination in poetry or prose. 'Eight Horses, Forty Men: 1914 War', written in September 1955, is the only poem that directly captures his wartime experience. Even then he takes us not to 'the Front', but a cold night in February 1918, when he is searching in the vast Le Havre railway yards with rifle and heavy kit for 'Dock 53' whence his troop train is to depart. Finally, through snow and hail he finds his train made up of box wagons with no windows or seats. On board, crammed in, he is taken to a 'destination unknown'.

ESCAPE FROM THE 'HORRORS OF WAR'

What does survive from this period is a collection which runs to over 250 pencil and coloured sketches and watercolours. The majority of these are set within the villages of Picardy. From where he was stationed he visited Varennes, Meaulte, Beauval, Warlincourt, Beauval, Villers-l'Hôpital, Masnières (which was completely devastated) and finally, after Armistice, Flixecourt. Many of his scenes are framed by open doorways, reminiscent of scenes he depicted in the years leading up to the war. Views partially obscured through doorways were an important tool he later used at Snowshill.

During the war, like during his schooldays, Charles would take himself off whenever possible on cycling sketching

Charles in his sapper's uniform in 1917.

master, where he made sketches in the villages of Lyddington and Stoke Dry.

It was not until late January 1917 that Charles was finally called up for training as an officer cadet at the Royal Artillery School in Topsham, near Exeter. His professional and financial standing qualified him for consideration as an officer, but during training the authorities apparently decided that he was not 'officer material', perhaps because of his unconventional manner. With his qualifications and carpentry skills he returned to the ranks as a sapper, rather than an unskilled pioneer. On 2 April 1917 he embarked for France as part of the

tours. His sketches in the villages were often quick and rough with annotations to record colours and other details that would later help him work up far more detailed drawings on tracing paper and with watercolours. After the war, 11 coloured drawings and seven pencil drawings were photographed for the architect and architectural historian William Henry Ward, to be included in his proposed book, *Battlefields of France*.

Ward was a friend of Mary Stratton, who had written *Bruges*. Fifty years old at the outbreak of the First World War, Ward had been determined to enlist and convinced recruiting staff that he was in fact 36. He was invalided back to England due to combat injuries but again returned to the Front. Wade's friend Harry Batsford was to publish *Battlefields of France* but this never happened, in part because Ward died in 1924 from post-operative complications resulting from his wartime injuries.

In areas where there was complete devastation and only rubble Charles had to rely on his memory and imagination for inspiration. He made a sketch of Betty Murray from memory and created imaginary scenes – little watercolours such as *Silent Pools*, *Garden Court*, and *Garden without Flowers*. *The Palace Garden* and *The Inland Sea* were two of the sketches that he 'imagined and made in a devastated area of France whilst on active service with a Field Company. … They show that it is possible to entirely escape from the most terrible surroundings in the midst of the horrors of war.' Many years later he would write a poem to accompany the painting *The Inland Sea*:

An utter stillness, ne'er a sound
Vibrates upon the calm all round
Such a strange etherial [sic] atmosphere
As an enchanted land of dreams.

Lyddington Hall, Rutland, **painted by Charles from notes he took in July 1914.**

not be rubbed down to a glass like surface.' The many mechanisms were to be electric – battery-powered, one assumes.

BEAUTY BORN OUT OF CONFLICT

On 16 January 1918 Charles left his unit on leave and travelled to England. Whilst in London Charles saw the painter Seymour Lucas RA, whom he had met at the Whitechapel House and Home Exhibition of 1911. Charles had previously lent Lucas a casque helmet from Farleigh Castle that he had bought a year earlier. At this meeting in 1918 Charles showed Lucas his sketches and paintings of French villages, on the strength of which Lucas encouraged Charles to apply for a transfer from the Workshop Corps to the Camouflage Section of the Royal Engineers. This new discipline was under the command of the painter Solomon J. Solomon FRA, to whom Lucas, a friend of Solomon's, soon wrote with copies of Charles's sketches: 'These leaves are from Wade's note book, whilst in the army in France, and I feel sure that you will agree with me in thinking that they are very remarkable and full of feeling and beauty.' This transfer never came about.

During this leave Charles also arranged for Amy to send some of his drawings to Uppingham School as part of an exhibition organised by Robinson. Robinson was able to report back to her that her son's drawings were 'much admired'. He said:

> [Charles] ought to be made an official war artist. I am sure he would make a better one than my other pupil – C.R. Nevison – whom I regard as three parts an imposter. But I don't think the horrors of war are in C. Wade's artistic line, so perhaps he is better off doing what he likes. I hope he is going to make a book of these drawings. It was such an enjoyable show.

A crucifix in a French village, painted by Charles in 1918.

Charles was particularly productive over Christmas 1917 and into the new year of 1918, drawing imaginary north European townscapes and landscapes. He also engaged in designs, and in June 1918 conceived a Byzantine mechanical cabinet in which figures moved about the space. He recorded that the work throughout the cabinet was to have a 15th-century feel and not a mechanical one: 'For example mother-of-pearl and gold on the palace walls will

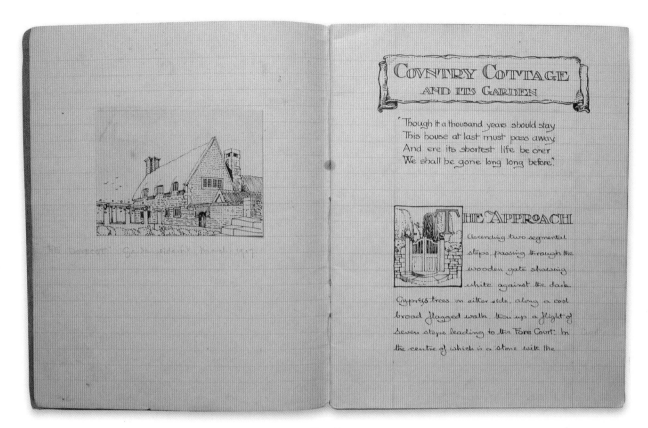

Before the war the size of Charles's collection had outgrown the confines of Yoxford and Temple Fortune Hill. More than storage space, Charles now wanted exhibition space to showcase his collection and to realise his architectural and decorative ambitions. Whilst there is no evidence to indicate that prior to the war he had been actively looking for a house of his own, it was clearly inevitable, and anticipated by the front door bell (1914) and model village of Fladbury. Charles's ideals for his house can be seen incubating in *The Country Cottage* manuscript (1907), the imaginative architectural schemes of 1907–09, and the text and illustrations for *The Spirit of the House* (1915). Service on the Western Front gave him time away from collecting and distance from home to consider the direction his life should take. In 1917 on a bookmark of his creation he put the motto, *Tempus est iam majore conari* – a shaky rendering of Livy's *tempus est*

etiam maiora conari: 'It is time to try even greater things.'

Whilst on the Western Front Charles came across a notice for the auction of the Snowshill Manor Estate near Broadway in the property supplement of *Country Life* magazine, dated 17 June 1916. It was one of eight lots to be auctioned off. Although the date for the auction, 21 June, had passed, Charles was determined to follow the manor's fate if he returned from the war.

Top: Pages from Charles's unpublished *The Country Cottage* manuscript. *Above:* Well Court, looking towards the astrological clock at Snowshill Manor.

5 The Spirit of the House 1919–30

With war over, Charles, having survived physically unscathed, was demobilised on 29 January 1919 and returned to England. Here he found that the manor house at Snowshill had not sold in 1916, but had been bought in July 1918 by William B. Driver, as part of a lot of 215 acres. Charles immediately contacted Bayleys, the estate agent, and learned that there was still an opportunity to purchase the manor.

AN ANCIENT MANOR

The manor of Snowshill is first recorded in AD821 as a gift from Coenwulf, the King of Mercia, to Winchcombe Abbey. After the dissolution of the monasteries in 1539 it passed into the ownership of the Crown. Henry VIII gave it to his sixth wife, Catherine Parr, as a wedding gift and on her death it passed to her last husband, Thomas Seymour. After his execution it fell into the hands of Edward VI, who presented it to the Earl of Warwick. Warwick's execution prompted its return to Queen Mary, before it was gifted to Francis Bulstrode in 1557. Perhaps unnerved by an emerging pattern of 'Crown, gift, execution, Crown, gift, execution', Bulstrode sold the manor to Henry Willoughby in 1561. It never returned to the Crown.

The earliest of the existing buildings dates from the mid-16th century. The additions to the south appear to have been built in two or three phases, by the Walle family and the Sandbachs, whose carved stone coat of arms

An illuminated manuscript page introducing the early history of Snowshill Manor.

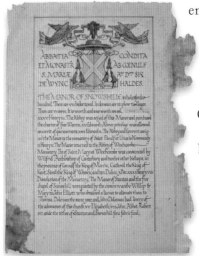

crowns the front door. The manor was subsequently occupied by tenant farming families, like the Marshalls, the Cooks, and lastly the Loveseys. Their alterations were minor and would nearly all be removed by Charles.

Charles visited Snowshill Manor in February 1919 and discovered, as advertised in 1918:

> An unspoiled specimen of an Ancient Manor House dating from the sixteenth Century. It is a characteristic example of the traditional mason work that the Cotswolds can show. The gables, mullioned windows, and simple chimney stacks make up a composition of great charm and picturesqueness.

Here Charles met the 'cantankerous old man' whom the owner had employed as a live-in caretaker. No doubt to extend his stay, contrary to the wishes of the owner, and without encouragement, he regaled to Charles a tale of the manor's impending doom as if to prevent a sale. As Charles recounted later, the old man warned him against climbing the stairs as these and the floors above were unsafe. He catalogued the manor's ills: it 'was all green mould' during the winter, falling masonry was a regular occurrence, and the 'rain poured in'. Rather than possessing 'great charm and picturesqueness', Charles was given to believe it tended towards the sublime – a fitting stage for a gothic novel. As it turned out, the sales particulars and the old man both exercised poetic licence in representing the manor, to further their interests. As an architect Charles could see for himself both the liabilities and the potential:

The property was in a most deplorable state of ruin and neglect, but had not been spoiled with modern additions. In spite of the gloom of the day and the desolation, I could visualise it as a delightful home.

Walking up the stone steps and through the front door, Charles entered the manor. The entrance hall had a panelled dado and flagstone floor. To the left was the dining room (now known as 'Turquoise') with an oak floor and oak-panelled walls. To the right was the drawing room ('Zenith'). Also on the ground floor was an inner hall ('Meridian'), a smoking room ('Admiral') and a cloakroom. Beyond was the kitchen ('Dragon'), then used by the caretaker as a storeroom and woodshed, and later used by Charles as a dining room and principal entertaining room.

Intending to convert the adjoining stables into the kitchen, Charles later removed the

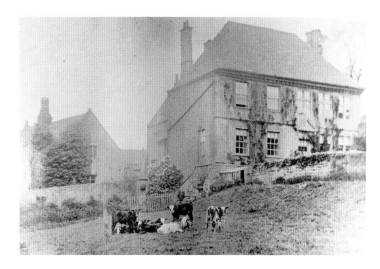

large range from the fireplace and found a few cubic feet of soot around it – hardly surprising, since it took a ton of coal a week to keep it going. The arched lintel of the fireplace and the chimney were in a 'precarious state' and required significant repairs. Between the sacks of onions and potatoes the exposed flagstone floor showed fresh scars consistent with using an axe

Above: Snowshill Manor in the late 19th century. *Below:* A plan of the ground floor at Snowshill Manor, drawn by Charles in one of his notebooks.

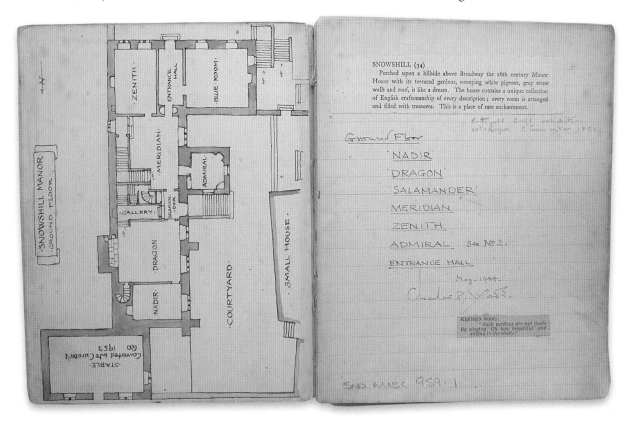

Zenith, showing Cantonese shrines, including Granny's cabinet. There are secret panels above the fireplace.

for log splitting. Here and throughout the manor rats roamed amongst the piles of rubbish the caretaker had introduced. It is ironic to hear now, given the quantity of items currently held in the manor, that the caretaker complained there was not enough space to store his belongings.

Off the kitchen were the scullery and the annexe (later joined to form 'Nadir') with 'a stone fireplace – a good example of the Elizabethan period'. From Dragon rose 'a fine old Elizabethan well staircase, having thick turned balusters and square newels, with shaped tops and pendants' (the 'Old Stairs'). Another staircase, the 'New Stairs', rose from Meridian to the first floor, and here at the southern end of the manor were four bedrooms (now three rooms: the 'Green Room', 'Occidens' [originally the 'Costume Room'] and the 'Grey Room') with floor-to-ceiling panelling and fire surrounds of a similar age.

There were another three rooms at the north end of this floor which had acted as bedrooms (later the 'Music Room', 'Ann's Room' and 'Seraphim'), most easily accessed from the Old Stairs. From here the Old Stairs climbed to the attics. This floor featured 'original doorways and doors' and a large attic, which Charles later called the 'Great Garret' (also known as 'Wheels Garret', and currently 'Hundred Wheels'). Under the manor, 'Excellent Cellarage' was to be found. Attached to the north gable, a hunting stable housed 'three roomy loose boxes'. Irrelevantly for Charles, the sales particulars emphasised that the property afforded excellent opportunities for golf and hunting, with the North Cotswold Hunt kennels located nearby at Broadway.

Charles wrote: 'The old house … stood sad and desolate in the midst of a wilderness of chaos, the result of long years of neglect'. Mostly unimproved since the 18th century, the manor, with 14 acres of land, three adjacent cottages and 'Lordship of the manor', was just what he had been looking for. Captivated, Charles

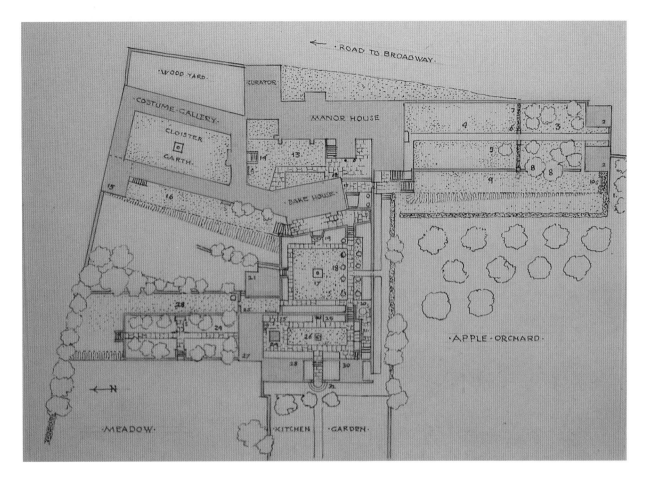

completed the purchase on 24 June 1919 for £3,500 (around £180,000 at today's prices). It is rumoured that, standing on the street, having just left the solicitors, a passer-by mistook Charles's unconventional appearance for someone who had fallen on hard times, and gave him some money for a reviving cup of tea.

'RECALLED TO LIFE': WORKING ON SNOWSHILL

Charles must have been bursting to begin work on the manor, but initially he continued to live at his old pre-war lodgings at Temple Fortune Hill, at least until the spring of 1920. Though his war service had prevented him from collecting, it had focused his mind on creativity – his only escape – and his future. He had been creative before, but Snowshill provided him with a new and greater intensity. Up until now, time and space had not allowed him to draw his various interests together. His life and collection were split between London and Yoxford, and the scale of his collection meant that his rooms in London and at Elmsley were storerooms rather than exhibition spaces. But now, for the first time in his life, Snowshill allowed him a backdrop to all his artistic pursuits. It gave him the chance to put into practice his philosophy on architecture, interior design and collecting.

Charles undertook extensive works on the house through the 1920s, using the stables adjoining the north end of the manor as a workshop. His plans for the house and garden were born of values and ideas that had been gestating since his childhood but had been rationalised since training

Charles's garden plan of Snowshill Manor, including the cloisters and tower that were never built.

Above: An enfilade of the ground floor at Snowshill Manor.
Above, right: Carvings in a niche in Meridian.

as an architect. His artwork, architectural designs and writings prior to the purchase of Snowshill Manor show this clearly. He wrote, 'always be very loath to destroy, save whenever possible, even at extra cost, extra trouble'. The cost, energy and time expended on the repairs to Snowshill illustrate his commitment to this. He used traditional materials and techniques whenever he could. Replacement stone was sourced from the disused quarry on the outskirts of the village – perhaps the source for the earlier construction of the house. To preserve the 'lovely undulating surface' of 'old plaster walls' repairs were undertaken using traditional wooden floats. Like John Ruskin, William Morris and the Society

for the Protection of Ancient Buildings, Charles asserted that one should respect later additions to an original building: 'Each addition is part of the history and growth of the house – learn to leave.'

Yet, like many others, he did not always practise the principles he extolled, and restoration was also a significant part of his work on the manor. Turquoise was left as the Sandbachs had built it, the only alteration being redecoration in turquoise (the Wade Blue already mentioned). The room now known as Admiral, similarly, was left alone except that a bow-fronted cabinet, 'an interesting attempt by a country carpenter at classic detail', was later built into one corner. In the Green Room, however, Charles removed the Victorian lowered ceilings and partition wall, and blocked a door opening, to return it to an earlier Georgian (not original) form. He filled in a Victorian door opening in the entrance hall and unblocked an older door in Nadir. He moved a wall in Zenith and Meridian, one between Ann's Room and Seraphim, and perhaps one between the Green Room and the Costume Room, to restore them to their original positions,

Turquoise (also known as the Blue Room), painted in Wade Blue.

and removed a Victorian partition wall in Nadir. In Zenith, Ann's Room and Seraphim he stripped back the coverings to expose earlier Elizabethan fireplaces. Here, he also removed lath and plaster to reveal the earlier open-joisted ceilings. Clearly Charles felt that he was revealing features that were more significant and provocative than those which obscured them. To this point his principles of repair, preservation and restoration are compatible with modern building conservation philosophy.

Nevertheless, his alterations to the buildings were not confined to restoration. With many building materials still in short supply as a result of the First World War, architectural salvage was both preferred and necessary to him. Previously, he had collected architectural salvage for its provenance, aesthetic merit and as authentic mise en scène for his art and portraits in historical costume; but now it

was for the repair, restoration and creation of new historical backdrops. He imported these elements from other historic buildings also to augment the atmosphere he had uncovered in the 16th- and 17th-century spaces in the manor.

Acquiring Snowshill brought him to a new stamping ground for collecting: from Russell & Sons at nearby Broadway he bought two nail-studded oak doors (now the doors to the cellar and cottage) and 103 feet in total of oak boards. He brought in Tudor and Jacobean panelling to line the walls of Dragon, Nadir, Meridian, Zenith, Seraphim, Ann's Room and the Music Room. In part their introduction may have been conjectural or simply motivated by desire. In all these rooms except the last he also installed oak shutters of his own design. In the Costume Room he introduced a door of a design he had seen in the French village of Saulty during the war.

The gardens at Snowshill Manor.

Charles also made alterations where he found the features, form and decoration aesthetically displeasing. For instance, the corridor leading to the Green Room was to him an unsatisfactory space. The ceiling was too high for the narrowness of the corridor, and rather than respect it as a feature of an earlier time, he created a barrel ceiling beneath it to produce more comfortable proportions. He made similar barrel ceilings in the Music Room and Nadir, using, surprisingly, plywood for panelling. He also enclosed the New Stairs, replicating the dado panelling to line the new walls; and he filled in the door opening on the first landing above 'Salamander' between the Old Stairs and the New Stairs because he felt that it was a draughty arrangement. Therefore, on completion, many of the rooms were a combination of three approaches: repair, restoration and creation. The layout of the house and garden that we see today is not the first design that he came to. It evolved. And some of his designs were never executed.

It is likely that the last alterations Charles made to the manor house itself were to the attics. Up to this point he had done little work to this area, although he had had to replace the floorboards of 'Spinning Wheels' (later called 'Top Gallant') and undertake significant repairs to the chimney. He had also removed the corn bins, 'riddled with wood beetle', from the walls of the Great Garret and inserted a dormer to replace the leaking skylight. Now, though, he inserted two new rooms up under the ridge above the nursery (later called 'Seventh Heaven'), nurse's bedroom (later called 'Top Royal') and 'Mermaid'. This work took place in the late 1920s and was probably not completed until about 1930. Access to these rooms was hidden behind a balcony Charles constructed towards the eastern end of the Great Garret, which could only be reached by a ladder through a trapdoor. The first of the two new rooms, for which he built a small dormer to light it, was called the 'Alchemist's Room' (now 'Witch's Garret'). Created as a piece of theatre to entertain his friends, it was also a tribute to Armagil Waad, Elizabeth I's advisor on alchemy, whose name invited a fanciful association with Charles's own that he did not discourage. In fact, the pentagram painted on the floor, so often referred to by those interested in the occult, is a symbol of good luck used by French Rosicrucians. He also painted a male and female mandrake on the plaster gable wall of the garret. The room beyond was never completed and remains unlined.

For Charles, Snowshill was 'not a museum', but a living and expressive architectural backdrop. He was determined to use the space and collection to provoke dramatic responses, tell stories and draw one back in time. He despised predictability, and used intrigue and mystery to fuel people's desire to move through one space into another. He built raised galleries in

Left: The Alchemist's Room (or Witch's Garret). *Below:* One of a pair of niche models of the alchemist, situated behind panels above the fireplace in Zenith.

Meridian and Dragon to give different perspectives on the rooms. Wherever possible, in the house and garden, he tried to avoid uninterrupted vistas. A hall, passage or room that dog-legged and disappeared around a corner was far more mysterious and curious than a space one could see from end to end. His later poem, 'The House', contrasts the 'sense of enchantment' in the 'fascinating way' of an old house with the soullessness of modern house design:

> Now corridors to boxes lead,
> Called rooms, in this drab Age
> of Speed.
> Each Box alike – but little change
> In rows like penal cells – they range.
> The Stairway but to reach next height
> Not one of fantasy – delight.
> Or may be Flat, no stair at all.
> So flattest dullness over all,
> No mysteries above, below,
> All that exists is there on show,
> There are but few who heed their loss,
> 'Tis Modern – so the best of course!

Charles would not live somewhere without a stairway, 'the most fascinating part of the house'. He regarded a lift or elevator as degrading, bringing one down to the level of 'the coals or the dustbin!' He praised:

A ghostly stair where secrets hide
Old cupboards built in walls each side,
A flight turns off – where will it end?
What awaits there round the next bend?

The cottage kitchen in the 1920s, after the insertion of a stone spiral staircase leading to Unicorn above.

He particularly liked the mystery of stone spiral staircases, and built two at Snowshill. One, in Dragon, was concealed behind a secret door in the panelling. In Meridian he

created another secret door in the antique panelling which gave access to a stone stair leading down into the cellars below. To Charles, doors were not simply devices to control passage between distinct spaces; they were there to invite questions about what was beyond. He used locked doors, secret doors and partially glazed or railed doors and gates to impede, tantalise and surprise the visitor.

If the stairs and doors were mysterious enticements through the house, patina and light also played an important part in the drama and spirit of the house and its collection. Patina from age is irreplaceable. It can only be earned, and must be venerated. It was a tangible link with the many spirits in the manor, a physical connection with the people who had once inhabited it. Years later Charles would plead for Ann's Room: 'The room has a lovely floor of silver grey oak in tone with the panelled walls, and it should be kept in its present state, not waxed or polished.'

The qualities of light were similarly cherished by Charles. During works to the manor he reinstated a window in Meridian, previously blocked up to avoid the window tax, and removed the cloakroom then covering it. However, quality rather than quantity was most important and in other rooms – Ann's Room, Zenith and the Costume Room – he left the windows blocked up, not only to preserve wall space for exhibiting, but to avoid a harsh cross light which would destroy the soft modelling of objects. It was not just the intensity of the lighting but also its colour and animation that he sought to control for best effect. Natural light was filtered through old (not modern) window glass, and candle and oil light through glass lenses or horn. Fire and candle light was used to highlight, shadow model, animate and distort architectural features and objects. Light and shadow were of equal importance to him.

INTRIGUE, MYSTERY AND MESSAGES

Text was another device Charles used throughout the manor and gardens to connect visitors with the space they were entering. The most obvious examples were the room names and mottoes he painted above the door lintels, mantelpieces and gates inside and outside the manor. As Charles repaired and altered the house and the arrangement of the collection from the 1920s to the 1940s, so the names of rooms also changed. Meridian was so named for being at the centre of the house between the two poles; Zenith, after the complement of suns or stars; Nadir, after the point in astronomy which lies directly beneath our feet. Salamander was named after the lizard-like creature that endures the flames of fire.

Dragon, the dining room with its great fire, was so named because traditionally dragons guard treasures and are so hot they cannot be cooled by water. The Grey Room, named after the light grey paint of the Georgian panelling, was originally called 'Columba Noachi' ('Noah's Dove') because from the window one could see the dovecote in the garden. Over the doorway of the Music Room (sometimes called 'Frank's Room', after a previous occupant) Charles painted the inscription: 'MAN IS CARRIED TO HEAVEN ON THE WINGS OF MUSIC'. In 1927 he gave Nadir a recessed frieze above the cornice, in which detached cast-lead letters, moulded by Charles from boxwood letters he had made by hand, form an inscription from Nicholas Breton:

Ann's Room and Seraphim beyond, with oak panelling introduced by Charles.

The Grey Room
(or Noah's Dove).

A WISE MAN IS LIKE A DIAL THAT BEING SET RIGHT BY THE SUN KEEPETH HIS TRUE COURSE IN HIS COMPASS. HE MEASURETH TIME & TEMPERETH NATURE. HE EMPLOYETH REASON, COMMANDETH SENSE & ENVIETH NONE.

Architectural use of text was common practice in the Arts and Crafts movement and many of Charles's earlier architectural illustrations employ this too.

THE COTTAGE

From the outset Charles regarded the manor house as a home for his collection and never for him. One of the great

Nadir, showing the lead letter frieze made by Charles.

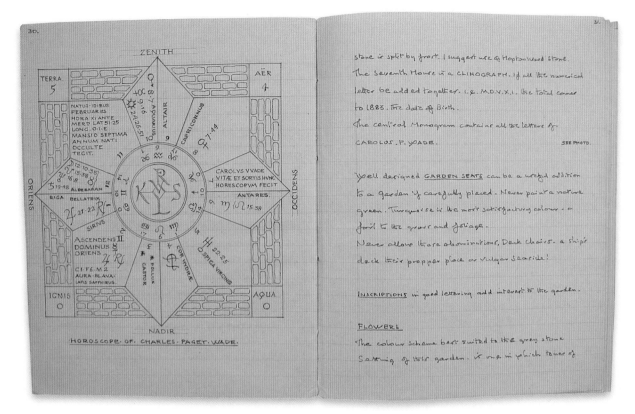

HOROSCOPE OF CHARLES PAGET WADE.

(diagram labels: ZENITH, TERRA 5, AËR 4, ORIENS, OCCIDENS, IGNIS, AQUA, NADIR, KPW monogram, CAROLVS VVADE VITÆ ET SORTIS HVNC HOROSCOPVM FECIT, ASCENDENS DOMINUS ORIENS, ALTAIR, CAPRICORNVS, ANTARES, SIRIVS, CASTOR, POLLUX, COR HYDRÆ, SPICA VIRGINIS, RIGA BELLATRIX, ALDEBARAN, AURA BLAVA, LAPIS SAPPHIRVS, NATVS IDIBVS FEBRVARIIS HORA XI ANTE MERID LAT 51.25 LONG O.I.E MANSIO SEPTIMA ANNVM NATI OCCVLTE TEGIT)

stone is split by frost. I suggest use of Hopton Wood stone.
The seventh House is a CLINOGRAPH. If all the numerical letters be added together. i.e. M.D.V.X.I. the total comes to 1883. The date of Birth.
The central Monogram contains all the letters of CAROLVS. P. WADE.   SEE PHOTO.

Well designed GARDEN SEATS can be a useful addition to a garden if carefully placed. Never paint a native green. Turquoise is the most satisfactory colour - a foil to the grass and foliage.
Never allow those abominations, Deck chairs - a ship's deck their proper place or vulgar seaside!

INSCRIPTIONS in good lettering add interest to the garden.

FLOWERS
The colour scheme best suited to the grey stone setting of this garden - is one in which tones of

---

attractions of the manor was the adjacent cottage, to the west across the courtyard. Bayleys' sales particulars termed it a 'fine original Retainer's House of the Jacobean period', until recently used as a 'Dairy, Brewhouse and Granary'. He found it 'in a deplorable state, smothered with ivy'. This cottage, which Charles sometimes called 'the Brewhouse', 'Priest's House' or 'Little House', was his own personal space. Although its arrangement was similar to the manor, the objects were chosen for his particular pleasure and their positioning reflected his compact lifestyle and domestic convenience. The earliest part of the building had two ground-floor rooms, where there had been a dairy, and two above. Charles made a doorway to connect the lower rooms, which became his living room and workshop. The first floor could be accessed by three sets of stairs. A set of stone stairs on the exterior divided the northern end of the 'Jacobean' cottage from a 19th-century stone addition. At the top of these was a landing offering views across the garden.

On the left of the upstairs landing was a doorway to the upper rooms of the original cottage, including Charles's bedroom. Now known as 'Griffon', he initially called it the 'Gallery Room', after a gallery he built to be able to see 'the lovely view to the west, across the deep valley to Littleworth Wood beyond'. On the opposite wall he fitted a box bed, with an oak-panelled interior containing two secret panels where he hid sets of drawers and a small electric light. Later, in 1929, he formed a shallow loft between two roof collars, and set a large crucifix of his own design and making there, perhaps inspired by those he sketched in the villages of Picardy during the war. It was flanked by a row of gilded French candle prickets set on a foliate crest. Below this, along the frieze of the loft, was an inscription borrowed from a church bell which read: 'Yesu for ye modir sake save al ye sauls that me gart make'.

The horoscope of Charles that he had carved out into the paving in the garden of Snowshill Manor.

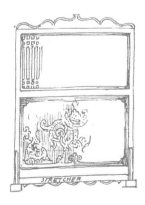

STRETCHER

leading up from the living room below. Not content with just this staircase, in about 1925 Charles had a one-armed stonemason build a second to Unicorn from the living room below – a candlelit, narrow, winding stone staircase. To the right of the landing at the top of the exterior stairs was the former coal house, open from the ground to the roof. In 1920 Charles built a ground floor for a boiler, to provide heating to Griffon and hot water for the bathroom above, which he created a second floor for. Rather than cut through the roof collar in the middle of the bathroom he built steps over it. He called this bathroom 'Balneary' (from *balnearium*, 'bathing place').

'ENTICING VISTAS WITH A HINT OF SOMETHING BEYOND'

Charles wrote of a garden, ''Tis man's rest, children's fairyland, bird's orchestra, butterfly's banquet'. Bayleys' sales particulars

An ink sketch by an unknown artist (above) and photograph (below) of the cottage kitchen at Snowshill Manor.

From the gallery in Griffon one climbed up another couple of steps, through a small door, to a narrow set of stone stairs descending steeply to the second room, which Charles had designated 'Betty's Bedroom' or 'Unicorn', for Betty Murray. The room also had a set of wooden stairs

of 1918 put a positive spin on the overgrown farmyard at Snowshill, which was criss-crossed with springs feeding a 'treacherous swampy morass' (Charles's phrase, not Bayleys'), waist-high in nettles and scattered with rusting and rotting debris: they stated that 'the Pleasure Grounds and Carriage Drive require to be formed'.

In 1920 the prominent architect Baillie Scott produced a preliminary design for the garden informed by Charles's demands. It is clear that Charles felt the eminent designer's involvement would result in a scheme of greater integrity than he might produce on his own. Baillie Scott only provided an initial layout, though. It was Charles who then set about fleshing it out,

Above: Griffon, Charles's bedroom, with the box bed in the corner.
Left: Balneary, the bathroom Charles built in the cottage.

Above: In Charles's time Sancta Maria was furnished as a baronial hall.

Right: A sketch by Charles of the interior of 'Jolly Roger', his second bedroom.

constructing terraces, stone walls, paths and sunken pools. The values seen in the house extended to the Arts and Crafts design of the garden, including a series of named outdoor 'rooms' with contrasting light and shade and moods. Here again, 'Mystery is most valuable in design: never show all there is at once'. Charles desired 'enticing vistas with a hint of something beyond' which drew the curious visitor through.

As much as he valued expertise in his garden designer, after his experience with the family gardener at Elmsley he decided he would never have a qualified gardener to care for his garden. To maintain his own authority and ownership he instead chose a hardworking man from among the builders, William Hodge, whose name and mauve hat were also to his liking.

After the initial works he set about fleshing out and ornamenting the new garden with interest, designing individual elements and features. In 1922 he bought a carved figure of 'Our lady' by an Austrian, Anton Dapre, making a niche dormer for it in one of the cow byres (which he called 'Sancta Maria'). He turned this byre into a pseudo-baronial hall complete with large banqueting table, walls lined with coats of arms, and funeral hatchments. At the east end of the open roof space he created a mezzanine bedroom ('Jolly Roger') which overlooked the baronial interior of Sancta Maria. Jolly Roger was simply furnished with a built-in box bed and chest, rush-seated ladder-back chair, a small chest below the window and lit with candlelight. Charles would sleep here when guests were staying in the manor and cottage in the summer months.

In 'Well Court', one of the garden 'rooms', he built two stone lunettes to house semi-circular panels, which he painted and installed in 1925. The largest of the pair, hanging below an astrological clock, is an excellent copy of a painting by the early

Renaissance artist Uccello, depicting the Battle of Egidio in 1416. Every autumn the panels were brought under cover until late spring, when the weather had begun to settle. In July 1926 Dapre carved him a wooden replica of St George and the vanquished dragon, and a decorative corbel for them to stand on, from a French original held at the South Kensington (now Victoria and Albert) Museum. Mounted on the exterior of the cottage, St George's arm is connected to a faceless turret clock which Charles installed inside Unicorn. On the hour St George struck the bell housed in the bellcote of Charles's design.

One of Charles's most intriguing and ambitious projects was an addition to the garden that never materialised. The proposed design included a gatehouse, cloisters and tower which housed a Byzantine-styled chapel and room set aside for his growing collection of manuscripts and early printed books. Its development and final design were much influenced by northern European vernacular architecture and detailing, like the cloister found in Lyddington, Rutland. The prototypes for the tower, cloisters and gatehouse can be seen in his illustrations of Alconbury Abbey (*c*.1907) and Kate Murray's unpublished manuscript, *The Strange Adventures of Nemo and Nulla* (*c*.1914). Unfortunately Charles did not have the finances to execute this ambitious architectural scheme at this time, and later, the shortage of building materials during the Second World War prevented its construction. With this went his only chance to build something designed entirely for himself.

The initial phase of works on the property lasted three years or more and focused on necessary repairs, structural alterations, restoration of earlier features and the installation of new elements such as linings to the buildings, and transforming the farmyard into a garden. Charles engaged

The wooden replica of St George and the dragon carved by Anton Dapre.

up to 28 workmen during this period, many of whom slept in the attics during the week. For one, the first night was the last. He had a visitation from the ghost of a Benedictine monk which village tradition spoke of haunting the manor.

'EACH HOUSE A MYSTERY SLEEPS'

Spirits of the house were not alone in keeping an eye on the workers. While work was ongoing at Snowshill Charles divided his time between the manor, London and Yoxford, and so he relied heavily on his foreman, W.A. Lewin. Lewin, who lived in the house during the works, appears to be a man of learning and imagination with an empathy for the manor and Charles. Lewin 'started sketching in oils in the summer evenings'. He wrote to Charles on 23 December 1921:

Drawings by Charles of coats of arms.

We have had a stormy week here and the wind has been howling and moaning around the house, and quiet subdued noises are heard in the house itself. And I sit, often alone in the house, painting, drawing, reading, or quietly thinking. I hear the subdued whisperings of the spirits which haunt the house, not wild … but … comfortable contented sighs, and whispers, as though the atmosphere in which they find themselves was congenial … I am glad we have been able to give them such a comfortable atmosphere and I flatter myself it speaks of the success of our work in the old house. I am sure when you return after Xmas you will feel the atmosphere of their visit radiating from the panels in the dining room, and elsewhere.

If these works were congenial to the spirits of the house, they proved less so to the incumbent caretaker, who was at last dislodged, as Charles described:

When I bought the place, he started the trick that his wife was too ill to move, encamped in the Blue Room. However when the workmen arrived they made matters so uncomfortable for him, clearing rooms of his rubbish, he was soon eager to move.

Charles was fascinated by the human history of the house and was keen to conjure up forgotten stories from its past. With Kate Murray's help he researched the previous occupants' coats of arms and had carvings made, which he painted and hung around the walls of Dragon. As a fatal sword duel was reputed to have taken place in Zenith, he hung two duelling swords above the fireplace in reference to the story. He heard the tale of Charles Marshall, a past tenant, whose ghost

met with a Richard Carter one night in the 1850s as the latter walked home from Hill Barn Farm (now Snowshill Lavender Farm). From that night on this ghostly companion, mounted on a black horse, rode beside Carter in silence during his walk home. Finally, on the advice of the church rector, Carter asked, 'What troublest thou, in the name of the Lord?' The ghost requested a meeting at midnight, when it gave Carter a message to pass on to his widow, Susannah. Carter complied, and divulged to no one but her the content of the message, which was rumoured to be the whereabouts of a hidden horde of money. The ghost of Charles Marshall was never seen again.

In 1920 during the repair of plasterwork above the doorway to a room off the Old Stairs, 'a very strange collection of odds and ends was found between the old studs'. This included hessian, clay pipe fragments, leather, pottery shards, animal bones, a buckle, stone, cloth buttons, cork pieces, turned wooden items and a scrap of paper bearing handwritten script. Hearing of a Brighton woman with 'a remarkable gift of seeing into the past and future', Charles sent her a fragment of an original roof beam from that room. He recorded:

She had never heard of Snowshill, but described 'Two houses set upon a steep slope, the larger lofty and mysterious, the other smaller and homely. In the larger house – an upper room – tis late at night, in it a girl in a green dress of the 17th century, much agitated, paces up and down. She does not live there, and will not stay the night.'

Charles subsequently discovered that in 1604, at a late hour on 13 February (Charles's own birthday), a secret marriage had taken place between Anthony Palmer and orphan Ann Parsons, then 15 years old. Ann was reputedly betrothed to the

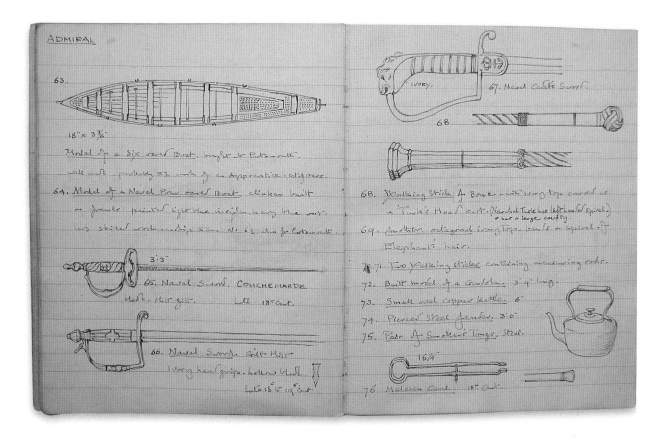

son of her guardian, Sir William Savage, but Palmer, brother to one of the household servants, pursued a successful clandestine courtship. That night he removed Ann from her guardian's house, Elmley Castle, and rode to Snowshill Manor where the ceremony was performed. Sir William retrieved Ann shortly after, and laid charges of kidnap and pursuing an unlawful marriage. Charles assumed that it was Ann Parsons whom the psychic had 'seen'. He named the room 'Ann's Room' for the girl who is sometimes said to haunt it still.

Over the years paranormal events have been regularly reported by staff and visitors to the manor. One day a cyclist asked Charles to tell him the order of the monk who had followed him up the Old Stairs. Ironically, as receptive as he was, Charles himself never saw a ghost, but Dotty Hands, who later worked for him, saw an unidentified hooded figure pass her on the Old Stairs.

FOR SALE?

In March 1924 the estate agency of Constable & Maude approached Charles to ask whether he would consider selling Snowshill Manor, one of a number of such enquiries he received during the 1920s. There is no evidence that he replied with a willingness to sell, but later that year there was a surprising development. In November Owlpen Manor at Uley, near Dursley in Gloucestershire, was offered for sale by Constable & Maude for £5,000. The Tudor Owlpen, like Snowshill, was constructed of Cotswold stone and limestone slates. The sales particulars mentioned 'the very fine timberwork, panelling and original open stone fireplaces'. Included in the sale price were ten acres of land, a traphouse, stables, a large cider mill house, an old corn mill and dam, and a stone-built cottage. Charles was interested and enquired about the expense of maintaining water supplies on

Pages from the Admiral room inventories.

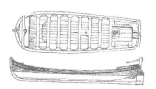

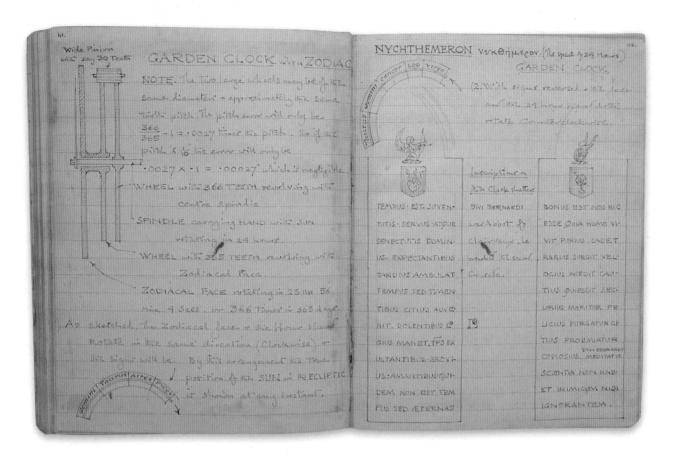

Charles's notes (above) about his astrological, or garden, clock. The clock can still be seen at Snowshill Manor (opposite).

the estate. He also arranged to visit Owlpen in mid-December, after which he went so far as to draft a written offer of £3,750 for the estate, subject to the completion of a surveyor's report and a contract approved by his solicitors.

Here the mystery begins. Was a formal offer made to Constable & Maude, or did he have second thoughts? Was his lower offer unacceptable to the vendor? No surveyor's report survives, so it seems not to have gone as far as that. What is certain is that the following year Owlpen was sold to the architect Norman Jewson for an even lower price of £3,200.

Through the 1920s the increasing beauty and eccentricity of Snowshill Manor and gardens attracted press coverage. The garden was used to illustrate the value of pools in the July 1924 issue of *Arts & Decoration*. In 1925 a photographer from *Country Life*

magazine came to Snowshill Manor on a pre-arranged visit.

In the February 1926 issue of *Homes and Gardens* the manor's kitchen and bakehouse (cottage kitchen), dining hall (Dragon) and bedroom (Ann's Room) were included in a section called 'Some Cotswold Interiors'. The caption for the cottage kitchen states: 'There is no make-believe about this interior. It comes down through the centuries.' A photograph of Snowshill Manor also appeared in the May 1927 issue of *Homes and Gardens*, noting that 'it is fortunate that so beautiful a house is in the care of an owner who has full appreciation of its character, and under whose guidance the fabric has been maintained with loving care'.

From the next decade on an increasing number of visitors would come to Snowshill, seeking treasure.

6 Artists and Literary Coves

From the early 1920s visitors became an increasingly significant part of Charles's life at Snowshill Manor. He was no stranger to interest in his appearance or costume collection prior to the war, but the number and variety of visitors who toured the manor now indicated genuine popularity. There were 501 visitors between May and August 1929, and 645 during the same period the following year. He embraced this renown, recording dates, names and numbers in visitors' books which survive for the years 1927 to 1946. These provide insight into the visitors, what Charles thought of them and reveal details of his own life during this period.

FRIENDS, FAMILY AND GUESTS

There were guests: family, friends and acquaintances Charles invited or who visited regularly. In the early years these accounted for the majority of his visitors. Most frequent among them was Frederick ('Fred') Hart, a lately retired lieutenant commander of the Royal Navy who would come to see his brother George in nearby

Chipping Campden and there met Charles. They struck up an immediate friendship which was to last for the rest of Charles's life, founded on their shared interest in hunting and collecting examples of craftsmanship.

Charles met Fred through Sydney Bolton Russell, a prominent resident of Snowshill who had purchased Tower Close in 1916, converting three cottages into one house. The owner of the Lygon Arms in Broadway since 1904, Russell had restored it to a coaching inn, where Charles bought many items of architectural salvage.

Russell had also bought the Snowshill Forge, derelict since the death of the last blacksmith, Charles Stanley, in 1909. Intending to preserve the building and its equipment, in November 1930 he showed it to a frequent guest at the Lygon Arms, the American car producer Henry Ford, who was looking for potential exhibits for his technology museum. Ford bought the forge and had it carefully recorded, deconstructed, shipped back to the United States and reconstructed in his Greenfield Village at the Henry Ford Museum near Detroit. On this visit Russell brought Ford to tour Snowshill Manor.

Charles became friends with other representatives of the local 'great and good' who were also owners of fine houses. There were the Milvains of Snowshill, the Dugdales of Sezincote and the Holland-Martins of Overbury in Worcestershire. Frederick Landseer Griggs, the eminent etcher and draughtsman, lived in nearby Chipping Campden and first met Charles to consult him on a design for the Snowshill war memorial. One of Charles's greatest friends, whom he must have met through London connections, was the architect,

Charles (centre) with Fred Hart (left) in the early 1930s. The third man is unknown.

academic, conservationist and collector Sir Albert Richardson. Charles had never hidden the fact that he was not an intellectual, stating that he had learnt little from books, 'a lot from pictures, but most from objects and skilled craftsmen'. Richardson, on the other hand, was an intellectual – though only too happy to put theory into practice. A highly successful architect, he moved in exalted artistic and architectural circles, opening the way for his presidency of the Royal Academy in 1954.

Of all Charles's friends, Richardson was the one who most shared his interests and tendencies. They both held strong opinions on architecture and the importance of their collections as a record of craftsmanship and the social values manifest in them. Whereas Charles's collecting was eclectic, Richardson focused primarily on the late Georgian period. Both men bought their treasure houses in 1919, but Richardson lived in his, and collected and arranged items to befit the domestic use of the large Georgian town house. Like Snowshill, Avenue House, Ampthill, had an 'untouched character' which captivated Richardson. It is said that in order to experience Georgian life, Richardson relied on candle, oil and fire for light and heat, refusing every encouragement to have electricity installed; he finally yielded to the wishes of his beloved wife, Elizabeth. From within the establishment he shaped the world through his writing, architectural designs and teaching of students. In comparison Charles lived in a far more personalised, introspective world.

Only family and the closest of friends were Charles's guests overnight. His sister Olive was a regular visitor, and every summer Kate and Betty Murray stayed from June through to early August, with Don joining them during that time. The artists Aldo and Eileen Cosimati, with their daughter Alda, were also frequent guests.

This group of friends entered into the spirit of the manor and Charles's world of make-believe with their own creative talents. Aldo sent Charles letters from fictitious authorities under fictitious letterheads.

Charles did not care much for guests cluttering up the bedrooms in the manor itself, and would only use the Grey Room, Ann's Room or Seraphim when there were too many to sleep in the cottage. Charles and his guests ate all their meals around the six-foot 17th-century oak table in the cottage kitchen, where the cooing of a pair of doves could be heard from a large wicker birdcage in the workshop. Their courtship often drove guests to distraction, and Charles would be forced to cover the cage in a sheet to cool their amorous behaviour. On the

Charles flanked by Kate and Betty Murray in 1934 at Snowshill Manor.

Charles makes repairs to the model canal bridge for Wolf's Cove in the 1930s.

Stencil design of a peacock on tracing paper by Charles.

bed with 'two flaming Flambeaus' which cast 'wonderful shadows'. Anne recalled that 'We slept, but the house never slept'.

Richard Kyle, who visited the manor in 1926 as a schoolboy, remembered Charles being a five-and-a-half-foot-tall man with sallow features and long hair curling around his ears (which his sister used to cut for him rather crudely). 'Crow's feet etched about the eyes and a long upper lip signalled an innate sense of humour', and he wore 'brown knee breeches, moleskin vest and Dickensian wing collar'. He had a reassuring voice of 'middle range with an educated diction'.

open landing beside the cottage peacocks would perch and peck those who ran the gauntlet to the bathroom or bedrooms.

A number of children were among Charles's guests in the late 1920s. Anne Powys-Lybbe, the daughter of family friend Henry Fretz (Fretts), recollected: 'He never changed, delicious long hair, breeches, long stockings, shoes with buckles, his dark eyes glittering with warmth, love and fun.' From the moment she and her brother arrived 'it was magic'. Charles would take the children around the manor showing them all of the items that had been added to the collection since their last visit, letting them dress in historic costumes and play with the prams and bicycles. They often sat in the workshop watching with wonder as Charles worked; they ate supper with wooden spoons and bowls by the large fire of the cottage living room. Then Charles would light the way to

His stance and mode of strutting about was like that of a ship's master pacing the quarterdeck. Bread he cut with disdain as if handling inferior stuff. Roughly hewn into chunks, he fumbled the crumb through his sensitive fingers with no thought of consumption. But jam he liked, guava jelly in particular, which he ate neat by the spoonful.

Charles was largely uninterested in food, and only basic cooking was possible in the cottage kitchen and workshop. Charles had an antipathy to modern kitchen equipment which he thought would undermine the ambience. Basic fare like bread, honey, guava jelly, omelette and stewed plums sufficed. On the mantle over the kitchen fire Charles had painted in the 1920s: 'God gives the food, the Devil sends the cook'. Meals were prepared for him and his visitors by women from the village, including Annie Hodge, the gardener's wife, and later Dotty Hands, who lived in the former Malthouse, one of the 18th-century cottages Charles owned across the road from the manor.

Richard Kyle also vividly remembered 'the sharp tang of turpentine and oil lamps' and the 'pungent smell of wood smoke' in

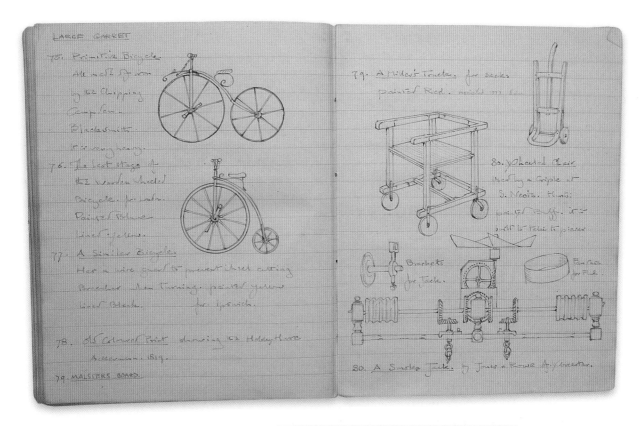

Pages from the Great Garret (Hundred Wheels) room inventory.

the cottage, and his surprise that the fire was well tended in the heat of July. Charles later told his friend George Dennis that this fire in the living room had not gone out since being lit in 1920. He often sat in his wooden, high, wing-backed armchair in front of the fire, reading a swashbuckling novel by Jeffery Farnol by candlelight or talking to a guest sitting opposite. If the fire was struggling, Charles, without leaving his chair, would simply reach above his head to slowly pull a weighted rope three or four times. The rope rose to a wooden wheel on the ceiling and then across and through the masonry wall into the workshop, where it connected with the arm of a great set of smithy's bellows. With a pull of the rope these would slowly rise and fall, pushing air through a nozzle into a small pipe which led back into the kitchen and under the embers to excite the fire in front of Charles. The appeal was as much about the ingenuity of a mechanical device, whose role was

The row of cottages opposite Snowshill Manor. Charles purchased the closest cottages with the manor. The National Trust now cares for the entire row.

The cottage kitchen today.

However, a minority were simply numbered under descriptors. He used the terms 'casualties' and 'strays' for visitors who happened upon the manor. Whilst these people were generally humoured, those categorised as 'intruders' or 'gatecrashers' irritated Charles by gaining entry over walls or through hedges and wandering unannounced into the garden. In such cases Charles did not feel compelled to be hospitable and was known to 'expel' them. He had two other, far more favourable labels, 'artists' and 'literary coves', which he proudly appended to the names of some of those who visited the manor.

Admittance did not guarantee all visitors the same tour. Some 'colonial folk', who had 'no knowledge of old things', made a tour very uninteresting and so Charles only gave them 'a short view – ground floor only'. Those considered 'very dull folk' might be 'banished' to wander the garden rather than see around the house. However, these were in the minority, and if Charles had the time and inclination he would turn provocateur and create a tour of drama and intrigue, telling stories, demonstrating 'bone-shakers', 'blood-letters' and serpents, and divulging the contents of cupboards and secret drawers. If one was really lucky, Charles would simply vanish during the tour. One scout, John Olive, later recalled how Charles 'used to disappear through the secret panel and then reappear behind us, which always gave us a start. He seemed a strange gentleman with his long hair, which, at the time, was so unfashionable.'

Directing visitors up the Old Stairs to Ann's Room, Charles would surreptitiously take the secret stone spiral stairs from Dragon to a landing where he hung historic costume on coat hooks. He would change into the costume and then leave the landing via a secret door in the panelling of Seraphim, where he seated himself to surprise the visitor.

surprising and not immediately apparent, as it was about convenience. Charles would ultimately pay for his love of open fires, lanterns and candles.

STRAYS

Increasingly, people asking for admittance to the manor had no prior connection with Charles. Many wrote in advance. These visitors sought entertainment and diversion, education and inspiration. They came in ones and twos, and in larger parties – 26 members of the Bedford Art Club with Richardson, 65 Oxford University students, or 37 furniture workers from Gordon Russell. In the 1920s and '30s the Holborn and Wimbledon scout troops visited the manor annually, camping in nearby fields. As more people owned cars Snowshill became a noted destination on Cotswold motoring tours.

Most individual visitors were named in the visitors' books by Charles – or by Betty, Eileen or Olive when they were staying.

and which had featured in a 1920 issue of *Homes and Gardens*. Now siting it along the north shore of the repaired and formalised garden pond, he transformed the landlocked Cotswold village of Fladbury into 'Wolf's Cove', a Cornish fishing village with luggers and navigational buoys. In the early 1930s he continued to develop Wolf's Cove with a canal and train system constructed by Espleys of Evesham, the building contractor engaged for many works on the manor. In 1931 John Betjeman produced an illustrated article on Wolf's Cove for his *Architectural Review*. His text and captions presented the village as if it was real, and many readers were temporarily taken in by the photographs of Charles's craftsmanship. Perhaps the most generous compliment came from Martin Hardie CBE of the Victoria and Albert Museum, who wrote to Betjeman that after coming across the illustrations for Wolf's Cove he had immediately decided to spend

Left: A self-portrait of Charles in the costume of a 'Corsican Brother', painted in *c*.1913. *Above:* A Florentine gilded cabinet. *Below:* Charles, Kate and Betty Murray, and members of the Rokeby School scouts in costume in 1927.

THE CALLING OF THE SEA

Although Snowshill is as far from the sea almost as any village in England, the manor reflects Charles's fascination with it, and its important place in the West Indian mercantile fortunes of the Wades and the naval careers of the Bulwers. Charles's great-great-grandfather Augustine Bulwer had been the chaplain on HMS *Theseus*, while his son (of the same name) owned a brigantine named after his wife, Bridget, and a yacht, the *Adelaide*. From the son Charles inherited a telescope, red ensign and model ships, and was inspired to collect more such objects, like a white ensign picked up from the North Sea by a First World War minesweeper, and Captain Oakes's sextant. Early on he put aside one of the most attractive (and smallest) rooms in the house for this collection alone. Originally known as the 'Admiral's Room', its name was distilled to 'Admiral'.

To further celebrate the sea in the garden, from 1925 Charles began to relocate 'Fladbury' – the 1:30 scale model village he had built in the garden of Temple Fortune Hill to entertain Betty Murray,

Wonderful Love: Caravan of Walter Grey of King's Lynn, at Blakeney, painted by Charles Wade, 1909.

his annual leave there; he only discovered the deception after failing to locate it on a map.

WORTHY VISITORS

Betjeman was not the only 'literary cove' to visit the manor in 1931. At the end of June the Poet Laureate John Masefield visited with his wife Constance. The same year, Graham and Vivien Greene moved to Chipping Campden. Vivien was introduced to Snowshill Manor by Kate Murray, and had coincidentally also become friends with Fred Hart. Perhaps her acquaintance with Charles and Fred helped fuel her later enthusiasm for collecting dolls' houses. The Greenes visited the manor on a number of occasions. Vivien believed that

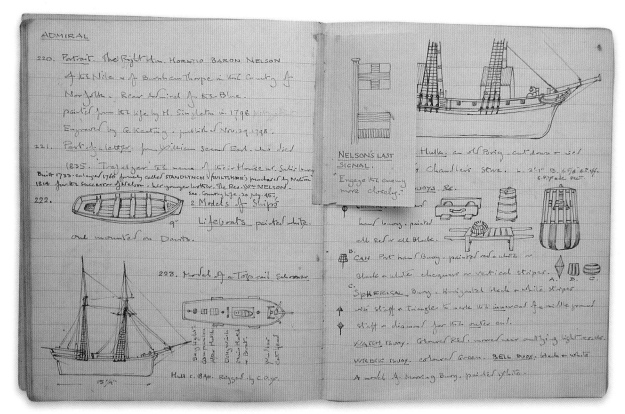

Charles was 'inhuman, half goblin half enchanter. He used to laugh to himself, rather disconcerting to a newcomer.' Her husband was less enamoured of Charles, as evidenced by his uncouth description of him: 'bowlegged in knickerbockers and bedroom slippers with dark greying hair bobbed over his shoulder, a blue striped shirt of the "gents haberdashery" kind and a black evening tie'. He remarked that 'he mouths his words and leaves them inchoate as though he was not used to speaking at all, and when he laughs at some rather obvious joke of a farcical physical kind he bellows like a child with open mouth'. It seems that Charles read aloud to the Greenes from his favourite author, Jeffery Farnol, 'making appropriate noises with pieces of old iron'. Greene's scorn for Charles was tempered by 'a terror that he was going to insult me with a suddenness which would leave me at a loss'. He at least admired the collection, which he felt was to Charles 'as much a toy as his model railway and village'.

Around this time John Fothergill visited Snowshill Manor on three occasions, after Richardson recommended it to him. He subsequently paired Charles's model village with Clovelly in Devon, describing them as 'two of the world's wonders'. Another notable visitor in 1931, the architect and writer Bertram Clough Williams-Ellis, went one up on Charles's model village to create the life-size Italianate village of Portmeirion on the Welsh coast. However, Williams-Ellis sought Charles's advice on mottoes for his gardens. Charles also provided him with a design for a cottage at Portmeirion, which was built at the end of 1931.

MODEL TRANSPORTATION

Charles loved traditional transport: carts and wagons were a noticeable subject in many of his sketches. Since Snowshill did not lend itself to exhibiting full-size examples of agricultural transport, Charles decided to obtain scale models instead to celebrate the skilful accuracy of the model maker as well as the craft of the wainwright and wheelwright. Whilst he was more than capable of making them himself, he was too busy, and instead commissioned Harold Robert Waiting to create 1:8 scale model wagons to represent each county in England.

The model fishing boat *John Silver* and other models Charles made for Wolf's Cove (left). Charles is seen placing the *John Silver* alongside the quay at Wolf's Cove in the 1930s (above right).

The Great Garret (or
Hundred Wheels).

Charles had earmarked the Great Garret in the attics as the wagons' exhibition space and built shelves along the eave line in 1932 to display them as Waiting completed them. As the years passed the collection of land transport grew to include bicycles, perambulators, a sedan chair, and an elaborately carved, painted and gilded full-scale Flemish chariot dating from 1749. It was winched up in sections through a trapdoor Charles had inserted above the New Stairs into Mermaid to get large items into the attics.

The large number of wheeled vehicles and contraptions inhabiting the Great Garret finally persuaded Charles after 1944 to rename it as Hundred Wheels, short-changing it. Unfortunately, Waiting died in March 1949, having only completed 17 of the planned model wagons.

STORMIER SEAS

At the beginning of January 1933 Charles left for St Kitts to inspect his Mansion Estate personally for the first time in 20 years. He made the trip with his mother, sister Connie and Fred Hart. Amy was still managing director of the family estates and, even in her advancing years, visited St Kitts far more frequently than her son. While there in 1935 riots broke out on the island, and Amy wrote to her sister Maud describing how a 'town mob' had intimidated estate labourers and set fire to the sugar cane crops, destroying 20 acres of Wade plantations as she watched. The police responded by opening fire on the rioters, killing three men and injuring eight. These violent scenes contrasted with Amy's description of life at the White House, 'so peaceful, four or five little white sails leaving for Nevis, a few hens parading about the garden, humming birds darting amid

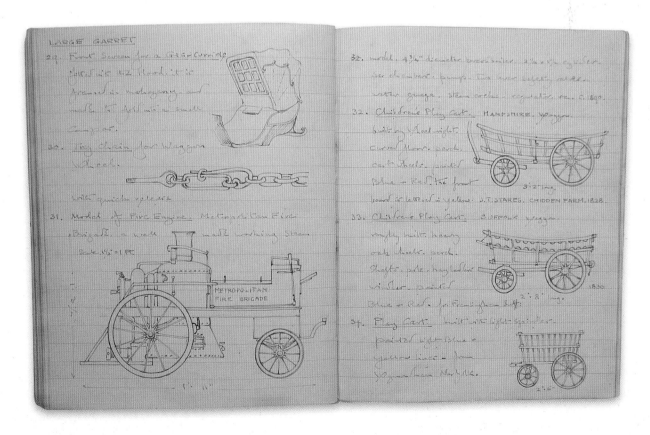

A watercolour of a fair at the Murrays' house in 1914, painted by Charles.

A painting by Charles taken from one of his notebooks.

the flowers and Baboo washing the two horses against the stable'. At the end of that year Amy reorganised the existing family estates into a limited company called Wade Plantations, appointing Charles co-director. She also gave over some land from one of the estates for the construction of a health centre for locals.

HOUSEWORK

It is clear from Charles's visitors' books that there was an 'open season' for visiting Snowshill Manor which ran from March to September each year with some stragglers received into October. In the quieter months Charles could concentrate on intensive cleaning, assisted by Dotty in later years. Starting in the cottage workshop, he cleaned his hundreds of tools and nests of drawers, and then moved into the manor to clean and re-display objects. Visitor numbers would then surge upwards with the passing of each month as temperatures soared and holidays beckoned. In September each year Charles began the task of putting the house and garden to bed for the winter. In the garden he brought the exposed painted panels and model village under cover. As the nights closed in, the temperatures dropped and moisture seeped into the manor from the rain, underlying springs and snow. Some rooms in the manor became uninhabitable for parts of the collection. Charles would often pack away smaller items so that they did not attract dust or damp.

COUNTRY GENT OR NECROMANCER?

The annual pack-up did not deter visitors. On 30 September 1933 the last of 811 visitors for the open season arrived: the novelist, playwright and broadcaster J.B. Priestley. Priestley described the interior 'as crazy as the outside, and as beautiful in its own way'. From the Costume Room 'you could have dressed whole opera companies', he recalled. He felt the cottage kitchen and workshop were reminiscent of early illustrations of Dickens' *The Old Curiosity Shop*. Of Charles he wrote that he had found one of the last of a famous company, the eccentric English country gentry.

John Buchan visited the manor first in July 1934 and in July 1935 returned with Virginia Woolf. John's son William observed that Charles had not just retired from London to Snowshill but 'he had almost left the century as well'. Woolf herself wrote:

> We went 40 miles to see a necromancer – that is a retired East Indian Planter who lives in a medieval farm which he has filled with old clothes, bicycles, mummies, alligators, Italian altars – not, I thought, very interesting, and I think rather a fraud, as he pretended to have no watch, and so I lost my train.

Charles did indeed have a large collection of clocks and pocket watches. However, he did not have a wristwatch and his love of clocks was not based on their telling the right time, but the passage of time; he celebrated their craftsmanship, the theatre of the cuckoo clocks and the atmosphere created by the tick-tock and the chimes.

If Woolf found Snowshill disappointing, there was growing evidence of its fascination

A 30-hour Dutch striking clock, *c.*1750, now in Seraphim.

for others: 1,357 people visited in 1935. The year before a young James Lees-Milne had visited the manor twice; he had long held a desire to protect country houses. After the speech Lord Lothian delivered at the AGM of the National Trust in 1934, imploring the Trust to find ways of preserving vulnerable country houses, gardens and collections, the Country House Committee of the National Trust was established, with Lees-Milne as its secretary. In this capacity he travelled through England and Wales (often on a bicycle) assessing country houses and encouraging owners of worthy piles to see the benefits of turning their houses over to the Trust. In this capacity he would soon see Snowshill Manor again.

7 'Today for me, tomorrow for you'

As Charles grew older he began to confront life after the manor, or, perhaps more uncomfortably, the manor's life after him. Tellingly, the motto painted above the doorway at the top of the New Stairs reads *Mihi Hodie Illi, Cras sed cui, Postea nescio* ('Today for me, tomorrow for you, but after that who knows?'). Having spent most of his life collecting, and the last 19 years investing much creativity, time and money in the manor and gardens, he would naturally have been appalled at the thought of his creation being lost after his death.

Many times he had seen auctions break up the prized collections of others, taking the opportunity to add to his own. He did not want Snowshill to share this fate, fall into 'the heartless hands of the auctioneer' and be dismembered to feed other people's collections. His thoughts turned to how he could secure its future. Aged 55, he was single (and seemingly unlikely to marry), with two unmarried sisters, no other close relatives or friends willing to take over, and no obvious custodian close at hand. A trip to St Kitts in January 1937 gave Charles time to think. Accompanying him were Fred, Amy, Connie and Olive. Soon after his return in mid-April, Charles wrote to his friend Harold Waiting saying that he planned to give the manor and its collection to the National Trust to preserve it for the nation.

PRESTIGIOUS VISITORS

A few months later, word of mouth attracted the attention of the highest office in the land. At 1.45pm on 30 July 1937 Her Majesty Queen Mary, with 15 lords and ladies, condescended to visit Snowshill. Surprisingly for such an accolade, Charles only ever recorded the visit in his visitors' book. The Queen wrote afterwards in her diary that she had seen 'an interesting colln of curios made by Mr Wade who showed us over the old manor Hse'. She was reported to have said that 'the finest thing in the collection was Mr Wade himself'.

Being a collector herself and champion for the Royal Collection, the Queen was renowned for seeking out items that had been loaned out but never returned. If an object of worth gained her attention during a visit an owner might feel obliged to donate it to the Royal Collection. Vivien Greene heard with amusement that Charles, forewarned, had hidden his favourite items, and that Queen Mary had 'struck a resounding whack at an 18th-century

Charles (standing) with an unknown woman (left), Revd Henry Jullion (centre) and Charles's sister Connie (right) in August 1937.

artefact with her umbrella, saying "That's a nice piece!"'

Following the royal seal of approval, Charles's efforts at Snowshill were further legitimised by a visit from the top of his own profession. In early July 1938 Edwin Lutyens visited Snowshill with a party of 11 from the Architectural Society. He recorded his impressions of the house and Charles in a letter to his wife:

> … a most remarkable creature, short, with a face like a death mask of Henry Irving topped with a thick fuzz of grey black hair, cut like a sponge! An untouched manor house, not one touch of modern grace, spotlessly clean save for the windows, thick leaded, small in deep reveals and then most creeper covered. … He is a most admirable craftsman, carves and draws beautifully and the whole house is a museum crammed, beautifully shown and arranged …
>
> He loves toys, has never grown up he says. I am told his bravery in the war was phenomenal. He must be in 'IT'. He has no servants, lives alone, one woman in the garden … and another woman does the house and keeps his enormous collection clean. The large amount of brass work and other metals are as bright as the sun and amidst all this collection in this ancient unrestored house 1500. He does not go out, lest he buy something he can't afford.

FOREVER, FOR EVERYONE

In August 1938 Charles formally approached the National Trust, outlining his concerns about the future of Snowshill Manor and its collection, and asking whether the Trust might be interested in owning them one day, after his death. At this time the National Trust possessed 45 historic buildings.

Charles Wade, painted by James Cramb from a photograph dated *c.*1954.

Charles Wade, photographed by Wenham Bassett-Lowke in the 1940s.

Looking through Meridian towards Dragon and Nadir beyond.

The Trust's Secretary, D.M. Matheson, replied that 'in view of its exceptional interest, [it] is, I am sure, the sort of place that ought to be preserved by the Trust'.

It was arranged that James Lees-Milne, already familiar with the manor, would visit the following Sunday. Afterwards, Lees-Milne wrote to Charles that the Executive Committee of the Trust was highly likely to accept Snowshill, but not without also securing the means to support it. He did not believe that admissions alone would be enough to maintain the house, collection and gardens in their existing state and therefore recommended that Charles make an endowment along with the gift of the manor. Lees-Milne felt 'so strongly that Snowshill should be safeguarded

permanently that we should make every effort for its preservation'. In response, Charles drafted a new will, bequeathing 'Snowshill Manor and its contents of ancient things ... Cottages and land belonging' to the National Trust. The rest of his estate was to be given to his two sisters in their lifetime and on their deaths 'to be used in the upkeep and any improvements the committee may deem fit at Snowshill'.

COLLECTING AND CURATING
Securing the future of Snowshill Manor and its collection appears to have given Charles confidence and a sense of justification in what he had created thus far; there followed a marked rise in collecting. If until now he had been collecting primarily to create historical domestic backdrops within the manor rooms, after 1938 this was almost abandoned in favour of the individual object. Charles's love of the hunt had not diminished. His later writings warmly express his delight in the characters he had met while collecting, and the places he had haunted – 'ancient attics', 'chilly crypts', or 'an eighteenth-century dancing academy'. He bought an English serpent in a greengrocer's in Aberdovey, a Florentine shrine from the top of a London bus, and a Spanish shrine on a ship in the mid-Atlantic.

Since he did not live in the manor and rarely used it to accommodate guests, domestic considerations did not curb Charles's ability to collect. A frequent visitor during this period would have noticed the dramatic change in the arrangement of the interiors as more and more items found their way into the manor. The superficial functions of rooms – bedroom, drawing room, parlour – became overwhelmed by the collection. Only Dragon, Ann's Room, Seraphim and the Grey Room fulfilled any real domestic role from the 1930s onwards. From 1937 even the Grey Room's role as a bedroom – and to a lesser degree Seraphim's

– was gradually overwhelmed, becoming an exhibition space which could also function as a bedroom if necessary.

Superficially, Zenith, Nadir and Mermaid were still reminiscent of a traditional though heavily furnished drawing room, parlour and bedchamber respectively. Mermaid, for instance, was arranged as an 18th-century English manorial bedroom. On the floor lay a Turkish and a Bokhara rug. A pair of mullion windows, which overlooked the dusty road and the row of Charles's cottages, and candle and rushlight lit this small attic room. Amongst the collection here was a pair of wood-carved angels standing upon carved acanthus capitals atop painted staves which came from Little Compton Manor in Warwickshire (these can now be seen on the Old Stairs). In the corner of the room (where a door now leads into Hundred Wheels) stood a four-poster bed hung with 17th-century hangings embroidered with animals and birds.

Against the wall an oak-cased cuckoo grandfather clock steadily ticked, and the walls were hung with oil paintings of the Virgin Mary and Jacobean men-of-war, painted silk funeral banners, and watercolours of ruins and trees. The furniture included an old winged armchair, 17th-century oak chests of drawers, a sideboard (which now stands in the Entrance Hall), a Flemish ebony cabinet and a Spanish cabinet covered in burnished gold leaf. Atop this stood a carved, painted and gilt bust of St Ignatius in the form of a reliquary (now in Meridian), two carved painted figures of bishops and one of a monk. Hide travelling boxes nestled on the floor beside and under furniture.

The room also housed a large collection of games, jigsaws, theatre scenes, children's stories and books of art instruction from Charles's childhood. The introduction of new objects was the most obvious cause for Charles's constant rearrangement of the collection, and forced him to find new

Right: A Spanish 16th-century reliquary of St Ignatius.

One of a pair of putti in Ann's Room.

ways of fitting large numbers of items into an increasingly small space. He wanted to avoid the 'disquietous and restless atmosphere' that many a crowded Victorian domestic interior created, and instead arrange objects 'with thought and care as to form one harmonious background'. He did this, freed from domesticity, by merging objects into the backdrop with 'subdued lighting', picking forms with shadow and 'golds and glints', and by attempting to focus particular types of object or aesthetics into particular spaces. It was his intention to create a perfect atmosphere of repose for the visitor.

The dedication of rooms to particular objects is seen especially in the attics, as in Hundred Wheels. The Lace Room was dominated by lace pillows, lace bobbins, bobbin winders and parchment patterns. The bobbins are decorative as well as functional, made of bone, boxwood, ebony, ivory and pearwood, and some are richly painted. Some have personal inscriptions, like 'Remember me Thomas Green' and 'Those who love me I will love. Ann Lovel 1840'. Charles considered these tools and those in other rooms as works of art in their own right.

The neighbouring room, Spinning Wheels, housed spinning wheels, as you might expect, and two large warping mills, one once owned by the silk warper Pleasance Webb of Sudbury, Suffolk. She sold this to Charles and told him that she used to give children rides on it as a roundabout. He noticed that her hands were deformed from working it. In the 1880s Pleasance had lived and worked with another silk weaver, Alice Housden, whose silk loom is exhibited in 'Mizzen' next door.

Elsewhere, notably in the Green Room, Charles attempted to group objects according to a cultural connection. Surviving invoices from this period show that Charles was now collecting a far higher proportion of oriental or Eastern-inspired items than ever before. Although the collection had always included items from the Middle East and Asia, the bulk of it up to the late 1930s was English or Continental. By 1944 he had emptied the Green Room of European items, and all but a 4000–3500BC Egyptian alabaster pot, the oldest object in his collection, were Chinese or Japanese. When the Green Room reached bursting point he was forced to relocate dozens of oriental items, shifting 24 to Zenith and 48 to Turquoise.

In 1939 Zenith had a strong Jacobean flavour. There was an oak court cupboard, refectory table, stool, wing-backed chair and hall porter's chair, studded leather coach trunk and two large 17th-century portraits. With the influx of Cantonese shrine cabinets and other oriental pieces these European items were all moved out into other rooms. Among the items shifted to Turquoise was one of Charles's favourite pieces of the entire collection: a Japanese figure carved out of a single piece of wood depicting a mask-maker at work, surrounded by his tools. Charles was in awe of the realism captured in the level of detail and craftsmanship. The figure has individual hairs inserted into the eyelids to form lashes. The musculature and pulsing veins are frozen in a moment of contemplation. The viewer is expecting this to be disturbed by the twitch of the eyelids, but it never comes.

Given the multicultural nature of the collection today it is easy to imagine that Charles travelled widely in search of treasures, but this is not the case. He did make a six-week motoring trip to Europe in 1930, with Fred Hart and Tom Bourne and his wife, and in 1938 he and Fred visited Java, Sumatra and Bali, where they collected examples of local craftsmanship including Balinese theatre masks. The vast majority of exotic items in the collection, however, had been imported into England many years before, as fashion and taste had dictated, and were now haemorrhaging from others' collections into Charles's.

One of the most striking parts of the collection is the 29 suits of Samurai armour. Most of these suits were found locally, out of fashion and out of sight during the Second World War. His first suit was bought

Above: Two spinning wheels in Top Gallant.
Left: The 19th-century Japanese carving of a mask-maker, said to be Charles's favourite item.

in December 1903 from the Old Cattle Market in Ipswich. This was to remain his only example for many years, locked in a chest. Years later, in search of a washer for a tap, he entered the tiny shop of the gasfitter and brass finisher Frank Thornton in Bennington Street, Cheltenham. Charles recalled of the shop:

A bookcase bureau styled as a Cantonese lacquered shrine for the European market, now in Turquoise.

It was so small, a sink and six taps filled its window. There standing by the counter was a set of Samurai armour! The owner said 'I have some more in the yard.' Outside he pulled off a tarpaulin and produced six complete suits that he had for 26 years. His wife would not let him have them in his house!

In a cellar in St Martin's Court, Charing Cross Road, he found a dirt- and dust-covered three-foot-high pile sold to him as 'debris, one pound'. This 'debris' gave up four complete suits of armour, including one of 'burnished gold lacquer' for a higher-ranking warrior.

Charles's collection is significant for containing not just ceremonial armour but battle armour of the lower ranks of the Samurai class. To show it all to the best advantage and produce a dramatic effect for the visitor, Charles made wooden articulating stands in the basic human form on which to hang the armour; some had faces with real human hair applied. Not all could be contained within the Green Room. One stood in the Grey Room. Three were set guarding the crowded and far more cosmopolitan collection along the corridor; this collection included a pair of

boots belonging to a postillion in the service of Empress Maria Theresa of Austria, discovered centuries after the postillion's death in a walled-up cupboard in his house.

A RETURN TO ST KITTS

In 1939 Charles undertook the most significant repairs on the manor since the early 1920s, and took a trip to St Kitts to supervise building works there. Earlier that year Wade Plantations' cotton production had been halted by the burning down of Spooners Cotton Ginnery. Due to shortages in building materials the ginnery was not actually rebuilt until 1943 and on completion the Wades rewarded their manager with a bonus. The strikes and civil unrest experienced in St Kitts and elsewhere in the West Indies between 1934 and 1938 had prompted the establishment of a Royal Commission, and when its representative visited Mansion Estate in 1939 he remarked that its people were far better off for houses and land than in Jamaica or any of the other islands.

KABUTO-NO-WAKIDATE
ZUNARI-NO-KABUTO
SIKORO
MABISASI
KEBIKI ODOSI
HANPÓ
SITUKESODE
SIHOBI-NO-O
SUGA
KUSARI = Mail
HOTOKEDO
TEKÓ
SINOGOTE
SUGAKE ODOSI
KOGAKE worn with straw sandle.
GESAN
ITAHAIDATE
Seal or Bear Skin Fur shoes.
ETTÜ-SUNEATE
TURANUKI worn 12-13th Cent.

The Names of the Parts of TŌSEI GUSŌKU

OYOROI = Great Harness
YOROI = the generic term for Armour.

The helmet and face mask of a Samurai warrior.

Javanese and Balinese theatre masks, in Seraphim.

Whilst staying there in 1939 Charles was overwhelmed by the generosity of his workers, who brought him daily gifts of eggs, vegetables and fruit. Very quickly he had 200 bananas in the house and 'a wonderful decorative display of various fruits at the end of the Dining Room'. Charles's view was not sanguine, though. As a traditionalist he was sad to see local headscarves being replaced with 'flashy cheap American hats', and the substitution of traditional building materials like shingles for concrete and corrugated iron. He wrote, 'the negro here is indeed a pathetic creature. We have robbed him of all his native traditions, and simply turned him into a mongrel, neither British or African.'

'SHADOWS FLICKER AS FLAMES BLAZE'

Future travel to St Kitts was halted by Hitler's invasion of Poland on 1 September

Above: A bronze hip mask depicting a leopard from Benin.
Below: German Augsburg marquetry cabinet, *c.*1560, now in Seraphim.

1939. The entry in Charles's visitors' book simply states, '12.45pm … WAR'. As wartime grain shortages caused the white flock of doves that Hodge had diligently maintained to give way to 'motley pigeons', so the period marked a gradual decline in Charles's way of life. This was punctuated by the deaths of those close to him, beginning with 'Dear Katie' (Kate Murray), who died on 11 October. Earlier that year, on what was to prove her last stay at Snowshill, Kate had fallen. After her mother's death Betty continued to visit, sometimes joined by Don, but now for days and weeks rather than months.

Shortly before this, in an intriguing development, a woman named Alison Coates had come to live with the 56-year-old, unmarried Charles. She slept in Betty's room. Charles taught Alison to use many of the tools in the workshop and she exhausted his large collection of Jeffery Farnol novels. The reasons for her stay are unclear – presumably related to the war – but it put both their reputations at risk. When this was pointed out by Mrs Hannay of Snowshill Hill, Alison moved out in May 1940. She continued to visit Charles after this, and later recalled the time fondly, albeit without recording anything to suggest a romantic relationship. Charles was often lonely after guests left, though he had regular contact with Dotty, Hodge and Fred.

The number of visitors to the manor declined at this time, though this was not entirely attributable to the war. It could have been because Snowshill was no longer a new attraction, or due to Charles's increasing focus on adding to his collection. He was not a recluse, however, and it should not be forgotten that even through the war he would see Dotty Hands every day, Hodge the gardener during the week, Fred at least once a week and throughout the year nearly one visitor a day, increasingly members of the armed forces. To those whom he did not know he was outgoing in his appearance, writing and actions, but less so in his conversation. It might be easy to conclude that, for all the visitors Charles allowed through the doors, he was by temperament a loner, but when guests like Betty or the Cosimatis left he always felt very lonely.

In May 1940, with an increasing threat of German invasion, recruits for the Local Defence Volunteers, soon to be retitled the Home Guard, were sought among men ineligible for the primary armed forces. Now 57, Charles volunteered for the Snowshill platoon, which met outside Sergeant Turner's shop in the village, and became responsible for camouflage. Out of hearing the rest of the troop called him 'Sir Charles'. Charles's long hair meant that his forage cap would not sit on the side of his head as it should – instead he had to drop the flaps and tie the cap on with string. It was also noticeable that his marching was slower than that of the others, but this was charitably attributed to the marching pace of the Royal Engineers with whom he had once served.

They drilled and trained on a Sunday and used the old quarry above the village as a rifle range. One day Charles was keen to fire the platoon's only Lewis gun and Sergeant Turner loaded three or so bullets into the drum magazine. Charles was about to lie down to get into the firing position when he lost his balance and fell forward – forcing the butt down and the muzzle skyward, and pulling the trigger in the confusion. On getting up he enquired if he had hit the target, and the sergeant replied that it was more likely he had hit men in the neighbouring village of Ford. Charles soon resigned, perhaps because of the physical exertion.

Charles's transport arrangements had always exercised a partial constraint on his collecting. However, even on a day trip to London by train he bought five cabinets and a bronze figure to the value of £81, to be delivered to him. The antiques dealer Roger Warner remembered Fred Hart's car, known as the 'Admiral's Barge', loaded up with the spoils of a successful day's antique hunting, chairs hanging to the outside from ropes. Charles told Warner that he had no car of his own because such mobility would enable treasure hunting on a scale he simply could not afford. When Fred and the 'Admiral's Barge' were unavailable he was reliant on other friends for transportation, especially George Dennis, who declined Charles's offer of a custodial role at Snowshill when the Trust took ownership. Dennis, a craftsman in his own right, completed a model of a medieval Gloucestershire farmhouse which he presented to the Trust in 1992.

The war and associated petrol rationing had little effect on the volume of Charles's collecting, which in fact grew, but did come to affect the range of his expeditions. In 1940 he visited many of his old treasure-hunting haunts in Norwich, Ipswich, Cambridge and London. However, the frequency of expeditions to more distant parts of the country greatly reduced as the war progressed. By 1943 excursions outside the orbit of Gloucestershire were exceptional and the number of dealers that Charles bought from dropped drastically.

Fortunately, in early 1942 Charles discovered the shop of (Albert) Wyndham

Payne in Portland Street, Cheltenham, which he could visit regularly by public transport. Surviving records show that between January 1942 and August 1945 Charles bought antiques almost exclusively from Payne.

Apart from petrol rationing, another reason for fewer long-range visits was the War Ministry's requisition of Elmsley, the family home in Yoxford, in early 1940. Amy and Connie decided to move much closer to Amy's sister, Maud, who lived in Wood Norton. They rented a cottage on the Wells Folly farm on the outskirts of Evenlode, near Moreton-in-Marsh, Oxfordshire. Olive had spent much of her life staying with relatives – increasingly,

Upper Mansion Estate yard, St Kitts, painted by Charles on his trip to St Kitts in 1910.

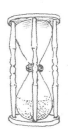

A snuff box made from coquille nut; the back opens to reveal a cavity.

as others passed away, with Charles. So Elmsley had to be emptied of its contents. Some items went to Wells Folly, a small amount to Snowshill, and the majority into long-term storage.

One of the benefits of Amy and Connie being turned out of Elmsley was that Charles was able to see much more of them. He was particularly pleased to be closer to Connie. In December 1941 Connie saw an eye specialist in Cheltenham because of a sudden difficulty seeing out of her right eye. Shortly afterwards Charles made a pre-arranged visit to Wells Folly and found her unconscious, having suffered a stroke as a result of ongoing high blood pressure. She died the following morning at 5am with Charles by her side.

Returning home Charles wrote on the last letter he had received from her: 'My dearest little Con's last letter.'

On Connie's death Amy gave up Wells Folly with the intention of living with Charles. Not surprisingly, being in her early eighties, she found Snowshill Manor uncomfortable and inconvenient. She had not had electricity at Elmsley, but still held rather higher expectations as to how one should

A Benjamin Pollock toy theatre, dated c.1824.

live. At Snowshill all but the most basic food had to be prepared off-site by Dotty Hands or Mrs Hodge. Here, in the manor and gardens, stairs abounded. To sleep in Unicorn meant using the cramped stone spiral staircase. The only toilet on the property, the Moule's Patent Earth Closet in Balneary, could only be accessed via exterior or interior stairs, an outside landing, peacocks, adverse weather and a further set of internal stile stairs. Built by Charles to avoid cutting through the original roof collar, he could have removed these stile stairs had he wished, but he did not. If his purpose was to discourage his mother, it was successful.

Describing Snowshill as 'too medieval' she took up Fred Hart's invitation to live with him in Chipping Campden. Even Charles conceded that Fred's house was 'most comfortably arranged' and 'full of interesting things'. Olive, nevertheless, continued to stay off and on with Charles rather than Fred and her mother. Amy appears to have been satisfied with this state of affairs but encouraged Charles to ensure he and Olive ate well. Like Charles, Olive was prone to not eating properly, and would later die from the effects of malnutrition.

In August 1943, whilst still living with Fred, Amy was admitted to Moreton-in-Marsh Hospital with heart failure. From here she was still able to write forthright letters filled with observations, requests and orders as chairwoman of Wade Plantations. In what was to be her last letter, she wrote to Charles saying that she hoped he had been successful at the last auction, but imploring 'no more Jap warriors'. In this final letter she drifted into reminiscence about croquet played on the lawn in front of the White House. Amy died in hospital on 25 August and was buried alongside Connie in the Snowshill churchyard. Charles designed her headstone, as he had done for his father and sister.

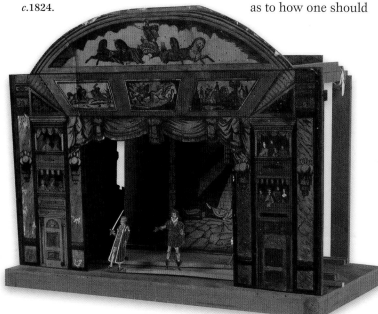

BAPTIST MEETING HOUSE   TEWKESBURY

Up small paved Alley-way, this little Chapel hides.
Within, an air of rare serenity abides.
Plain whitened walls, grey Gallery. Old Pulpit tall,
Through windows set with old green glass, soft shadows fall.
Firm RULE held sway — no VANITIES ïer entered here.
The only "sparkle" came from BRAZEN Candelier.
Stern Sermons clearly pictured FIRE and BRIMSTONE FATE
Of All who were without this Chapel's sacred STATE.

Amy's death was felt deeply in St Kitts, where for many she was more than an employer. Since taking over the mantle from her husband in 1911 she had been an astute and well-respected head of Wade Plantations – and of her family. In response to her death Charles called an extraordinary meeting of the company directors: himself, Olive and Fred Hart. At this meeting Charles moved and was supported in changing the company articles to install himself as Governing Director of Wade Plantations Limited. This position, for life, gave him almost absolute powers to appoint and remove other directors of the company. Olive and Fred had become company directors by receiving shares in Amy's will. Fred's autobiography did not disclose what shares Amy gave him in recognition of his services to her and the company; nor did it reveal details of his company directorship or role as St Kitts representative to the West Indies Cotton Growers Association – though it does record his view, with hindsight, that this industry, of which the Wades were a part, exploited its workers.

The Wade business had suffered during the war: the cotton ginnery in Montserrat had been destroyed by fire; in the middle of 1941 the Sendall and Wade offices were badly damaged during the bombing of the City of London, and early in 1944 the Labourers' Union and the Planters' Association were engaged in negotiations over raising the minimum wages, which led to an unofficial strike across St Kitts. Mansion Estate labourers continued to work until hostility from other striking workers forced them to stop. Perhaps their loyalty was due to Charles's managers, staff bonuses, and continuing contribution to a Labourers' Savings Scheme. This did not prevent the Wade estates being subject to the suspicious fires that were affecting other estates across the island in March 1944.

Pages from one of Charles's notebooks depicting a coastal scene and the Tewkesbury Baptist Chapel.

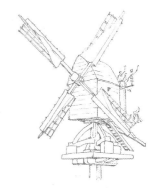

'HAPHAZARD NOTES'

Charles's mother's death must have left him, at 60, feeling exposed. No doubt he saw more clearly his own demise, and that his creative time was limited. So, in 1944, with Snowshill bequeathed to the National Trust, he set about in earnest to compile an illustrated room-by-room inventory of all its objects. These were not simply lists but filled with individual ink drawings, descriptions of use and appearance, and sometimes included the price and the place of purchase or family connection. The following year he also embarked upon his memoir, *Days Far Away* (published by the National Trust in 1999), and *Haphazard Notes*, which included poetry and observations. These were followed in 1946 with a notebook given over to personal reminiscences of Yoxford which show that he believed his life history would benefit future visitors to Snowshill.

Pages from one of Charles's notebooks.

Charles wrote of his journals that these 'in years to come some use may be, as aid into the past to see'. He added that, 'though a jack of many trades, and though being in touch with literary folk, I have never attempted to write till quite recently, turning to thoughts of my earliest days – doubtless a sign of old age!' The inventory and notebooks show how important it was to him that the National Trust and future visitors understood the collection and the life that formed it. He wished these journals to remain at Snowshill in the Gallery Room (Griffon) 'where the last rays of sunlight fall … so long loved home to me'.

MEETING MARY

The war in Europe ended in early May 1945. A month later, on the day of the village fete, 16 June, Mary McEwen Gore Graham went walking through the gardens

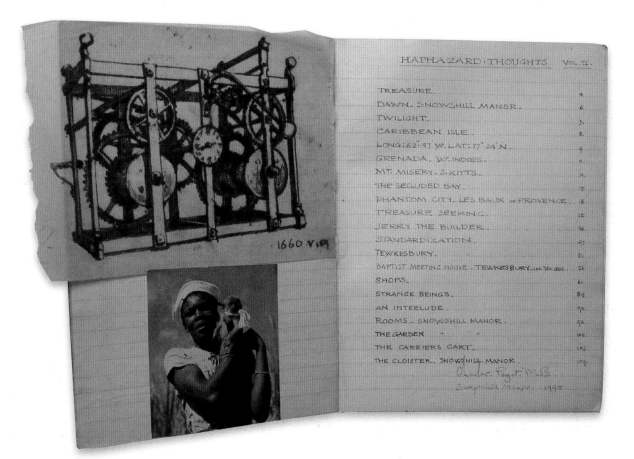

and came to the cottage. Here she recalled seeing a 'strange little figure coming down the steps. He looked most odd, I apologised and said "This must be private", Charles replied "It certainly is!"'

Charles, at 62 years of age, had just met his future wife. She was of comparable height to Charles at five feet four inches tall, with green eyes and golden wavy hair. Born in Worcester in 1902, Mary was the eldest of three children, with two younger brothers. Her father, Revd (Edward) Percy Gore Graham, had originally worked as an accountant but was ordained a priest in 1908. Prior to his ordination he had been an agent for the British and Foreign Bible Society in Malaya, becoming a deacon in the Philippine Islands and licensed preacher for the Diocese of Singapore in 1905. In 1924 Percy became the rector of St Michael's Church, Eastwell, in Leicestershire. Mary's mother, Alice Anne (*née* Smith), had married Percy in 1897 and they are now buried together at Eastwell.

Like Charles, Mary had attended boarding schools as a child: the Clergy Daughters' School in Bristol and then Boxgrove School in Guildford, Surrey. During the Second World War she went to live in Broadway, at the vicarage and then at Fairview House. She found employment with the furniture company Gordon Russell Limited, making the model aeroplanes that were essential for training the Royal Observer Corps and the armed forces in aircraft recognition. When she met Charles she was working as a waitress at St Patrick's tearoom in Broadway. Charles later offered to approach one of his friends in Cheltenham in order to find more suitable employment for her, away from 'forks, food and feeders'. It was whilst living in Broadway that she decided to visit Snowshill Manor on the day of the fete.

Mary's youthful appearance and liking for fashionable clothes was in direct contrast to Charles's archaic look. However,

Mary McEwen Gore Graham as a young woman.

she evidently exercised an old-fashioned feminine prerogative to be imprecise about her age. Her birth certificate announces her arrival in the world in 1902 but on her marriage certificate in 1946 she owns up to a mere 34 years.

During their first conversation Mary mentioned to Charles that she was fond of writing and showed him her endeavours at his request. He then asked if he could show some of her poetry to Betty Murray. Mary asked Charles not to, as she was 'shy' of her poetry. He was himself increasingly writing poetry and over the next few months they swapped poems.

Poetry was a new creative outlet for him. Dwindling visitor numbers, Amy's death and his own sense of mortality may have contributed to this new passion. He had used poetry in his art and architectural designs, and had encouraged Betty to write

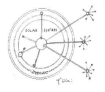

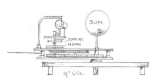

letters to Charles appear to be hopeful of a future together:

> I wonder if it would be possible for 2 people to live together and never speak – just to know by Instinct, Intelligence and Intuition!
>
> What lovely moonlight nights they are now. I picture the scene over the valley to the woods from your window.

In early September, on hearing that Betty was to visit, Charles invited Mary to join him and Olive for supper, and to meet and show her poetry to Betty. After this Mary became a regular visitor to the manor, visiting four times in October, as well as meeting Charles in Cheltenham. There was a further visit to Cheltenham together, and six visits to the manor in November. During their courting Charles was certainly very much in love with Mary and signed off letters with declarations like, 'I adore you'.

'I GIVE MY HEART TO THEE, FAIR MAID'

On Friday, 21 December 1945, 'the most wonderful of days', whilst sitting next to the fire in the kitchen of the cottage, Mary and Charles said they loved each other and agreed to marry. He told her that he had longed to love and cherish somebody.

Whilst Charles seemed self-sufficient, choosing to live on the periphery of society, he had relied on a chosen few throughout his life to provide companionship and counsel, particularly Connie and Amy, who were now dead. Olive, who survived them, was loving but required care. Before he met Mary there is little evidence that Charles had ever pursued any love interest in his life, despite society's suspicions concerning Alison Coates.

A tantalising undated draft letter to an unnamed recipient seems to show Charles

An imaginary north European walled town, painted by Charles whilst staying in St Kitts in 1910.

poetry as a child, but he had never pursued it seriously himself until late in the war. Between 1945 and his death in 1956 he produced nearly 40 illustrated notebooks which were dominated by his poems. He favoured narrative poems which captured parts of his own life or conjured up stories of life and death, ghosts, pirates, seaside inns and smugglers. He once remarked: 'Alas (in whatever field) when accomplished how far short of inspiration, my works fall – yet somehow, this fact is an urge to attempt yet again and again.' Charles's poetry is valuable more for giving ready access to his thoughts, opinions and values than its artistry.

Mary came to visit again in late August and met Charles's surviving sister Olive. Just two months after first meeting, her

Above, left: The pond at Snowshill Manor.
Above: A pen and colour wash by Charles of a Caribbean street scene.

turning down marriage on the grounds that he was not a safe bet and that his financial situation was unfavourable at that moment in time. Could this have been intended for Mary, or for a mysterious earlier liaison? Given the close and longstanding friendship with Betty, who remained unmarried up to the time of Charles's marriage, one might suspect him of being interested in her, and it is said that Kate and Don Murray had once seen Charles as possible matrimonial material for Betty. However, when Charles and Mary's engagement was announced Betty expressed great relief that he had finally got his 'domestic arrangements on a reasonable footing'. She had been concerned that Charles's continued secrecy, impractical in a small village such as Snowshill, about his ongoing relationship with Mary had made him vulnerable to scandal. She offered to assist with the wedding ceremony in any way she could.

Charles began to plan alterations to make the cottage more comfortable for Mary. His strength of feeling for her – or, perhaps, his own advancing years – prompted domestic improvements that his love for his mother four years earlier could not. By summer 1946 he was writing to Mary of his pleasure at the thought that after '40 days penance' the cottage 'will be your home as well as mine'.

Charles and Mary married in the Cheltenham Registry Office on 5 September 1946. Without any fuss it appears they took the village bus from Snowshill to Cheltenham to their wedding. Not marrying in a church is perhaps surprising, given that Mary's father was a vicar, but Charles was not a churchgoer and did not like weddings. He believed that they were personal affairs which were ruined when hijacked by the associated labours and post-wedding festivities. If at all possible he had avoided attending them as a guest. Of those he did attend, one he arrived at late because he had been 'ensnared by an antique on the way' and the other was his own.

8 'When my spirit's fled away' 1946–56

Looking back, Fred Hart and others saw Charles's marriage to Mary as the end of his previous way of life. Fred would have reasonably expected that his friend would remain a bachelor like himself, and after the marriage 'never felt the old intimacy again'. The marriage had less effect on Richardson, whom Charles had only ever known as a married man; he had married Elizabeth Byersin in 1902.

The match came as a complete surprise to George Dennis, who recalled:

Design by Charles for a house in Montserrat, West Indies.

DESIGN FOR A HOUSE IN MONTSERRAT, WEST INDIES, BUILT OVER THE VAULTS OF AN 18TH CENT SUGAR MILL. A COMPLICATED MASS OF SLAVE BUILT MASONRY SOME 80 FT DIAMETER AND 12FT HIGH. C.P. WADE. A.R.I.B.A.

One Saturday Mr Wade invited my wife and myself to Snowshill to see his latest acquisition. He prepared tea, consisting of bread an inch thick with slabs of butter on them. Then a lady walked in and we were introduced to his 'latest acquisition', his wife!

Charles and Mary settled into married life in the cottage. It must have been a snug existence, if somewhat basic. The galley kitchen was dark and cold; cooking was done on oil stoves. There was no electricity but Mary insisted that a telephone be installed. To accommodate her, Charles built her a swing chair, which still hangs from the kitchen ceiling so that it is positioned at the head of the dining table, and had Espleys of Evesham build a wardrobe at the end of her bed. They slept in separate rooms – Mary's box bed was in Unicorn, while Charles slept in Griffon next door – but their relationship was romantic. Mary reminisced that when Charles mowed the lawn she would sometimes position herself at one end in order to reward him with a kiss whenever he turned the mower around.

CHARLES AND MARY VISIT ST KITTS

Charles and Mary had not spent six months together at Snowshill when, in February 1947, they left to spend more than a year in the West Indies. Not since the days of his grandfather and uncles had a Wade stayed continuously for this period of time. During the war the White House had been cared for by Lydia ('Lyd') Nias, a 'live-out' housekeeper and esteemed former companion to Amy and Connie. Henry Jullion, now archdeacon, lived there for a period too. Charles's 1947 visit was perhaps

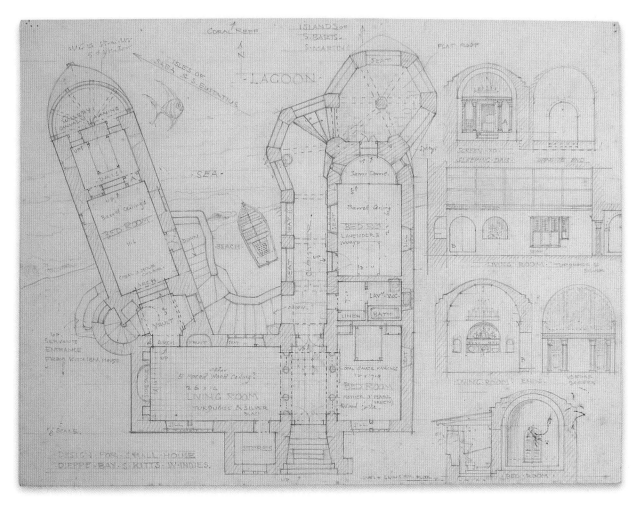

intended to serve as a trial for a permanent move, and may have inspired him to prepare various designs for a new St Kitts residence. One was the conversion of the windmill on his lower Mansion Estate yard, and another was for an entirely new stone beach house in Dieppe Bay, where Charles owned land and a derelict house bordering the beach. The third was the conversion of a ruinous old stone cotton mill, 80 feet in diameter, on his estate at Mill Farm in Montserrat. None of these imaginative designs was ever executed, and Charles and Mary remained at the White House.

In the past Charles and his parents had split their time between the 'country house' at Upper Mansion and the 'town house', the White House, outside Basseterre.

However, by May 1945 Mansion House was considered 'merely standing' and uninhabitable for any length of time. This was in part due to the shortages during the war, which had prevented Mansion's manager, Arthur Evelyn, from obtaining nails to repair its buildings, let alone install the lavatory that Charles had requested.

The house's perilous state could not be attributed simply to the war, though. In 1883 a Banyan tree had been planted close to the house to celebrate Charles's birth. As he grew up and visited St Kitts he came to love these trees deeply, depicting them in his artwork and later writings. As this particular Banyan grew and matured it spread out and, with the support of aerial prop roots, began to threaten the Mansion

Design by Charles for a small beachfront house in Dieppe Bay, St Kitts.

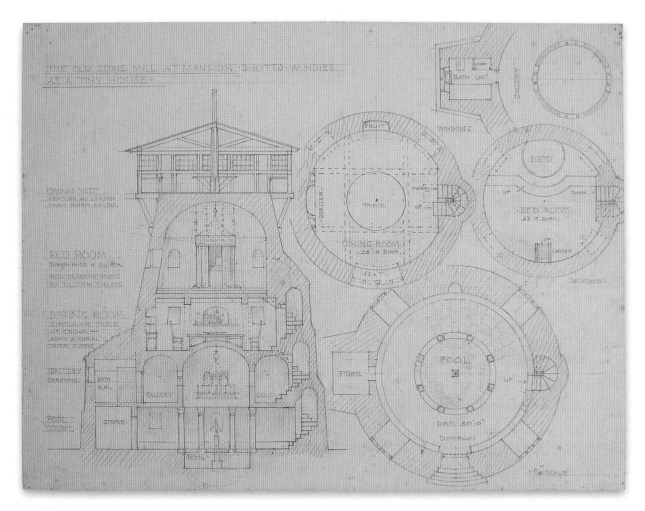

Design by Charles for an Old Stone Mill at Mansion Estate, St Kitts.

House. Evelyn recommended that the tree be cut down but Charles refused, and ultimately this led to the destruction of the house. In 1952 he wrote a poem about the tree as it engulfed the Mansion House.

Charles's lifestyle at the White House was far more modest than that of Amy, Paget, Edwin, Henry or Solomon before him. The cellars stood as a sad testimony to this earlier period when the house, permanently occupied, was the social and economic heart of the sugar estates' management. Since then they had been forgotten, and were now only frequented by rats, scorpions and spiders. Yet they still housed bottles, casks, flagons, and hogsheads filled with champagne, moselle and other wines which, alas, many years before had turned to vinegar and were

now leaking from the corks. Similarly, the coach house still housed a chaise with green coachwork from the days of Queen Victoria, which Amy had used on her last visit to St Kitts in 1938. Amy and Paget, when not on horseback, had used this to tour the estates when staying here. Now it was slowly decaying. This was the story of many of the objects that Charles had collected over the years. They too, once necessary, had fallen into obsolescence and obscurity.

Charles loved the White House and its setting. The house had verandas on three sides. Here on hot days he could retreat to swing in a hammock, caressed by a breeze laden with the sweet smells of fruit trees and flowers. He could look across the countryside to Basseterre and the glittering

Caribbean Sea beyond, and dream. This was the parallel to sitting in his hall porter's chair with winds moaning in the chimney, wood smoke in the air and firelight dancing on the walls of the cottage at Snowshill. One of the verandas looked down into the courtyard that lay between this and the detached cookhouse. In the sun-drenched courtyard, hummingbird and dragonfly hovered amongst guava and cinnamon trees. The windows and doors which opened out onto the verandas had painted jalousies (blinds) of emerald green. The chickens would nest in the mango trees.

Life was not entirely carefree. Charles, more than ever before, was intimately connected with the day-to-day business concerns of Wade Plantations Limited. In England, all Wade Plantations business was filtered through the London offices of Sendall and Wade. His residence in St Kitts changed who was at the end of the communication, though he still chose to rely more heavily on the estate managers than his mother and father had before him.

The business also continued to be troubled by periods of unrest. In 1946 Spooners Cotton Ginnery had been subject to a three-week strike by workers demanding a one-hour lunch break. In January 1948 a three-month strike began, promoted by the President of the Trades and Labour Union of St Kitts, Robert Llewellyn Bradshaw. A persuasive orator, determined champion for the working class and dangerous opponent of the plantocracy, Bradshaw would later become the first Premier of St Kitts. His threat to planters can be seen in the letter that Mary wrote to the Colonial Office stating that Bradshaw was a 'public menace' bringing 'danger and disaster ... upon this Island', and calling for him to be deported or brought under stricter control. Between January and July 1,500 acres and 45,000 tons of the Wades' sugar cane were destroyed by arson.

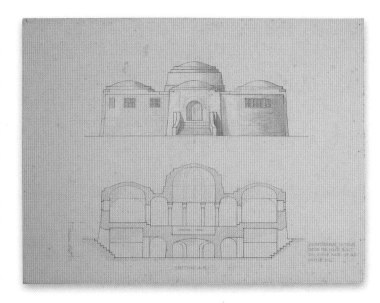

TYING UP LOOSE ENDS

At the end of January 1948 Charles and Mary left St Kitts and toured the Caribbean islands for four months before returning to England and completing the sale of Elmsley in June. Parting with Elmsley would leave Charles without a home for the six coaches and carriages he had stored there. He had intended to display them in his projected 'cloisters' development at Snowshill, but with no immediate prospect of this, and with Elmsley sold, he urgently offered

Design by Charles for a house in Montserrat on the base of an old cattle mill.

A ballpoint sketch by Charles of the cellar at the White House in St Kitts.

An imaginary European coastal walled town, painted by Charles.

Charles's depiction of the encroachment of Banyan trees on his Mansion Estate building.

them to the National Trust for display in another of its properties. Lees-Milne's agent inspected them and found them to be 'extremely dirty, tarnished and rusty', and noted that necessary re-upholstering would be difficult and expensive. Charles, believing them to be 'interesting records of a highly skilled craft, now gone forever', countered that Lees-Milne had taken a rather 'gloomy' view of the carriages; he declared that the upholstery of four of them was in 'quite a fair state' and should not be replaced as the 'old quality of braid … is quite unobtainable today'. But with little choice Charles gifted the six early carriages to the National Trust.

As it turned out, the Trust was unable to house them and Charles resignedly asked if it could find them a good home. Eventually they were sold to George C. Mossman of Woodside Riding Stables, near Luton. Some of Charles's collection, along with Mossman's, is now housed at the Stockwood Discovery Centre, Luton.

In recognition of this offer and gifting of the manor in his will, Charles was made an Honorary Member of the National Trust in June 1949.

MARY AT SNOWSHILL

Back in Snowshill, Mary set about finding her place in the village. She became a churchwarden for St Barnabas and on one occasion whilst she was away she left important keys to the church in her 'third drawer', which Charles wrote to say, somewhat dramatically, had prevented christenings, marriages and deaths. Having bought a Worsley car from Connie's estate, after petrol rationing had eased, Charles employed local man Frank Gunn to chauffeur him and Mary. Gunn was allowed to use the car when they did not need it, until Mary, in Charles's name, abruptly requested its return. On returning the car documents it seems Gunn was surprised to find that Charles was ignorant of his wife's order, although unwilling to gainsay it.

In the garden William Hodge had been in charge since the beginning of the 1920s. Charles and Hodge were contemporaries, being born (and later dying) in the same year. They had clearly formed an understanding over many years, grounded on more than Charles's appreciation of Hodge's mauve hat. With Hodge's help Charles had created a garden he could be proud of, avoiding what he called 'a nurseryman's triumph – artless shame', or 'open acres with rows of flowers without any shade or mystery'. Hodge even rented the land below Sancta Maria for his own large vegetable garden.

It is possible that Mary thought Charles needed to take a firmer hand in the running of the garden. For example, she wanted Charles to stop turning a blind eye to the village children scrumping for apples in the orchard. However, Hodge saw this intervention as interference and in the early 1950s he had an exchange with Mary in which he told her what he thought of her and left; he had been the Snowshill gardener for more than 30 years. Dotty's husband, Vic, became the gardener in his place and remained so until about 1964 when William Hodge's son Robert took over for the next 15 years.

At the beginning of January 1950 Mary went on holiday by herself to Malta, via France and Italy. On the way she lost her tickets twice, which Charles described as 'gross carelessness'. She made the most of her time away: in Malta she attended a polo match graced by Princess Elizabeth and the Duke of Edinburgh; she went to the Malta Garrison Ball; and among her papers is an invitation to the St John Dinner, addressed to 'Miss M Gore-Graham'. Her letters to Charles during this time communicate what a wonderful holiday she is having. With very few visitors, Charles relied heavily on Dotty, her village news, and the wireless radio programmes 'Much Binding in the Marsh' and the 'Brains Trust'. He was also kept company by a kitten and a painted wooden chimney cat, which Richardson had once gifted to him.

Charles's letters to Mary were full of news of the village, his work on the manor

The cat, a gift from Sir Albert Richardson, whose whiskers Charles had to regularly replace.

The gardens at Snowshill Manor, as kept by William Hodge.

and gardens, and rationing. They also show his longing to have her back and, increasingly, his frustration with her. On 20 February he wrote asking when she was coming home. On 1 March he wrote, 'What are you up to. Tis far too long since I had news.' On the 5th he wrote that he had every right to be very angry about her constant requests for advances on her Wade Plantations directorship fees. On this occasion he sent her half of the £100 she requested, and warned her it was the last advance. This letter so infuriated Mary that she tore it up, but later taped it back together.

In a letter dated 14 March, Charles scolded her for her ingratitude and failure to advise her return date from Malta. He added:

Your 'difficulties' are easy to understand – you spend more than you have got and continually expect me to fill the gap. I have been very patient, but cannot continue. You knew what money you had, and should have planned your stay accordingly. This seems a ridiculously expensive holiday.

At the end of April he wrote, 'please do not disappoint me again, by having no passage booked. Expect you 11–12th [May] at latest.' Eventually Mary returned home, at the end of May.

In late October Charles and Mary returned to St Kitts, via Quebec. Back in St Kitts he made a reluctant visit to the local Apollo cinema with Mary. The seat had no covering, the mildew on the screen gave the heroine measles, and the dialogue was frequently drowned out by 'the audience below', some of whom were 'forcibly removed'. The final straw was when Mary fainted in horror as the villain of the piece drew a blood-stained knife on the heroine.

Also on this trip, at the age of 68, Charles commissioned another portrait of himself from Mrs K. Browning, the wife of the vicar on St Kitts. His commission was intended to instil confidence in her as an artist, but unfortunately the completed work did not instil confidence in him as a patron or subject and he gave it away. The subsequent owner later repatriated it to Snowshill after Charles's death. Nevertheless, years later Mary expressed a hope that it would be removed from the manor as she believed it gave a false impression of her husband.

A GIFT TO THE NATIONAL TRUST

In the years leading up to 1951 Charles was becoming increasingly worried about his business and finances, writing with envy of the dolls in his mother's doll's house, who 'were free from all our troubles' and lived in Elysium. The maids of that house never gave notice or 'dreamed of wages'. There, 'fashions never changed', 'pipes never burst' and no work was needed. The dolls had no worries about taxes which, Charles complained, were absorbing all his money. Mary was concerned as well and wrote to their lawyers, Lee & Pembertons, to ask about having Charles's property transferred to her to avoid the 45 per cent death duties on his personal estate, which was then valued at £107,000. Anthony Leathart, their solicitor, replied to Charles himself and counselled against Mary's proposal. Instead, knowing that Charles had gifted Snowshill Manor and its contents to the National Trust in his will, Leathart suggested that he hand everything over sooner to avoid his estate paying

higher death duties. This should then be conditional on the Trust allowing Charles and Mary to reside in the cottage for the rest of their lives.

Charles took this advice and at the beginning of 1951 prepared the 'Deed of Gift' to the National Trust, writing that 'I [have] achieved at Snowshill Manor what I set out to achieve as a very small boy'. Leaving Mary in St Kitts, Charles returned to England by himself in April 1951 to make the preparations for handing the manor over. He passed his architectural books on to George Dennis, and gifted more than 250 pencil and coloured sketches and watercolours, which he had made whilst on active service in France in the First World War, to the Royal Institute of British Architects. Charles returned to St Kitts on 20 October, recording his occupation as

The portrait of Charles by Mrs K. Browning (1881–1978), c.1950.

A watercolour by Charles for *The Spirit of the House* by Kate Murray, 1913. Note the use of Wade Blue on the gates.

inspected on behalf of the Trust in 1938. Between September 1938 and 1951 there are surviving invoices for the purchase of at least 1,569 further items, not counting the 400 or so items from Elmsley. Whilst Charles's marriage, and his money worries, had greatly curbed his collecting in the last five years, he did not stop entirely, even after giving the manor to the Trust. In fact, Roger Warner remembers Charles visiting his shop after leaving Snowshill for the last time as owner on the way to Southampton, en route to the West Indies. He spent £1,500 which, among other things, secured a portrait of Henry VIII.

Warner was instructed to deliver these items to the manor. His reception bearing these gifts was frosty and he recorded: 'I think myself – and Henry VIII – were both very nearly lynched in the courtyard for bringing another load of items that they had nowhere to place.' The Trust felt unable to open the manor as it was and turned to Fred Hart to help them rearrange the collection. Fred remained the honorary curator until Herbert William Maxwell took over later in 1952.

The official National Trust opening of the manor was on 3 May 1952. Charles and Mary stayed in St Kitts. Charles's reasons for staying away are not documented, but it is clear that it would have been an uncomfortable occasion for him. Guests arrived in the driving rain and the ceremony was conducted in Turquoise while a storm raged outside. The flickering candlelight picked out the guests and cast animated shadows across the room.

A DIFFERENT KIND OF LIFE
Far away in St Kitts, Charles's life had become decidedly more sedentary and withdrawn. At Snowshill he had kept busy repairing, polishing, entertaining, or treasure seeking further afield, but at the White House he began to observe 'Ambition's relentless spirit

'estate owner' and his permanent address of residence as St Kitts.

The manor Charles gifted to the National Trust had changed considerably from the property Lees-Milne first

A coastal landscape painting, possibly by Charles.

die'. Now his time was largely filled with rest and nostalgia.

Whilst the warmer climes had always forced a change in his wardrobe, it scarcely tempered its more archaic excesses. Modern men's fashion gave Charles not the 'slightest passion'. His winged collars, woollen jackets and knee breeches were replaced by white linen, and his head crowned by a straw broad-brimmed hat which in England had only been brought out on the sunniest of days. Beneath it, his shoulder-length hair, once dark brown, was now almost entirely grey and rounded black- or faux tortoiseshell-framed glasses regularly rested on his nose. He assumed the appearance of a member of the island plantocracy, but from the reign of Edward VII, so that Kittitians still considered him 'eccentric' and 'out of keeping'. Mary liked to hold parties, but Charles disliked the 'chatter' of 'trivial things of no account', where 'nought that's said will ever matter'. After one particular party, freed from its 'ghastly turmoil', he vowed never to attend another.

He was much more at ease writing or drawing or swinging from his hammock on the veranda, 'with the sweet fragrance of the flowers' floating on a 'whisper of [a] caressing breeze'. His bedroom, like the rest of the house, was sparsely appointed in comparison to his Snowshill cottage. The walls were painted a sea green and the ceiling, open to rafters, ivory. The furniture here was mostly inherited with the house – a dark mahogany regency chest with a mirror, two Victorian ultramarine glass candlesticks and two small Staffordshire dogs. Atop the bureau was a gilded Burmese figure and 18th-century model frigate. There was an 'ancient' canopy bed with the posts made out of mountain wood to a local design, a few old paintings of English country scenes and a collection of books – old companions, like Dickens and Pepys. The only regular disruption to Charles's life was on Saturday when, in his words, the 'philistines attack my room', to clean it. Charles hated this as it upset his train of

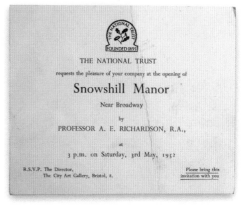

THE NATIONAL TRUST

requests the pleasure of your company at the opening of

Snowshill Manor

Near Broadway

by

PROFESSOR A. E. RICHARDSON, R.A.,

at

3 p.m. on Saturday, 3rd May, 1952

R.S.V.P. The Director,
The City Art Gallery, Bristol, 8.

Please bring this invitation with you

An invitation to the official opening of Snowshill Manor as a National Trust property in May 1952.

The nautical theme of the collection in Admiral is clear to see.

thought and everything was moved about. The evenings, the 'Magic hours', were his favourite time of the day.

Charles spent his days and nights writing poems, acutely aware that 'time speeds away'. His poetry produced an unexpected benefit: that of helping Mary's insomnia when many different medicines had failed. He would give her his notebooks to read and after a few minutes she would say, 'Charles, I really must go to bed'. Some of his poetry, like 'Yesterdays, Todays, Tomorrows', considered the passing of time, directly and indirectly; ticking clocks were a recurring character in many of his narrative poems, just as they were in the mise en scène of the manor. Contemplating his own death, he asked life to 'ease our parting, steal away' and let death 'linger not – give little warning'. In 'Survival' he voiced his hope that his memory, 'In written word will linger on'. He was not foolish enough to think that his words' value to others was a certainty. But they were certainly valuable to him:

These humble lines that I have penned,
An aid to happy memories lend,
Though nought they may to others be,
Yet sacred they have been to me,
For they have called to life again,
Some well-loved scene, some sweet refrain,
Some fragrance from the faded past,
[…] Some echo that would peel away,
Recaptured for a longer stay,
Some thought, elusive as a sound,
Hath by the written word been bound,
  And when my spirit's fled away,
    Tis my behest that these books stay,
      At the ancient manor of Snowshill,
      Such is my testament and will.

Some Staffordshire dogs that reside in the large doll's house in Mermaid.

Though Charles was growing old and his limbs were 'tired and feeble', he was able to 'let [his] imagination roam'. These poetic excursions took him back to childhood haunts in England and overseas, but also to places and times he had only ever visited in his imagination. Common to them is his certainty that older buildings and objects act as receptacles of past experiences they have borne witness to. Consequently, he writes with great sadness about a forlorn building which stands waiting, yearning 'for days it can ne'er regain, for voices long fled away'.

A COSTUME DRAMA

Charles's nostalgia had not entirely displaced dreams for the future, though, and he continued to hope that his cloisters development might be built in the grounds at Snowshill. While handing the manor to the Trust, he had stopped short of gifting perhaps the single most important part of his collection: 1,200 pieces of historical costume. He nonetheless continued to store

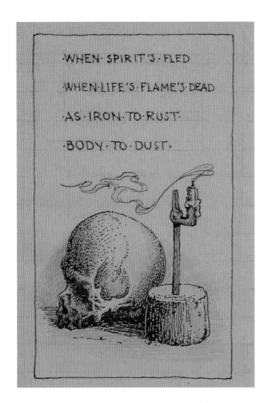

·WHEN· SPIRIT'S· FLED

·WHEN·LIFE'S· FLAME'S· DEAD

·AS· IRON· TO· RUST·

·BODY· TO· DUST·

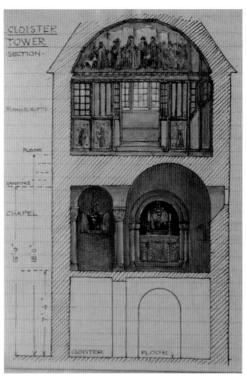

Far left: The endnote to one of Charles's notebooks.
Left: Pen and ink cross-section of Charles's unexecuted cloister tower.

them at the manor, which suited the Trust. It had always seen the costume collection as a jewel in the Snowshill crown, and was hopeful that Charles would, in time, look upon the Trust as a worthy recipient. There were other interested parties, as Charles did not forbear to tell the Trust. It was perhaps painful for Lees-Milne to be informed by Charles that the new costume curator for the Manchester Museum felt that his venue, which borrowed a large number of costumes for their Festival Exhibition of 1951, would be the best home for them. Storage space in the Costume Room (renamed Occidens by the Trust) was limited, the garments hanging in large glazed wardrobes.

Finally, in December 1952 Charles offered the costume collection to the National Trust, on the condition that the Trust agreed to build a gallery befitting its exhibition. When the Trust saw his detailed design for the gallery it quickly realised that it was part of the far larger cloisters complex which Charles had first designed in the early 1920s: a two-storey tower or garden house at the north end of the grass terrace, with 'a magnificent view over the Vale of Evesham'. Consciously or unconsciously, the costume collection became Charles's bait to entice the Trust into realising this ambitious building project.

The project remained in the Trust's management plan for the property until the 1990s but was never carried out, largely because of the capital outlay required. The collection has been displayed at the National Trust property of Berrington Hall, Worcestershire, since the 1990s.

OVERDRAWN AND OVERSEAS

In May 1953 Mary returned to England without Charles, who remained in St Kitts furiously writing his poetry. Mary's mother had broken her leg and it had been surgically pinned. With Mary's father having died in 1949, she decided to collect her mother and bring her to St Kitts, to convalesce with them during the English winter. To help

An imaginary
European coastal
walled town,
painted by Charles.

her with this task she brought West Indian Peter Neale Daway, who travelled first class in a separate cabin. On the ships' passenger lists Daway is described as an 'agent', but Mary treated him publicly as hired help and a chauffeur for the Worsley. He was a friendly and caring man but impractical, and therefore was seen by Snowshill's curator, Maxwell, as more of a hindrance than a help.

Mary clearly thought a lot of Daway and as a widow in St Kitts she would come to rely on him heavily. After he died abroad she had his body brought back to the island and a concrete mausoleum built for him in the graveyard of St Peters, near the White House. It is said that when he was interred she could not bear the tomb being sealed, and was forcibly removed from the graveyard to allow this. Soon after Daway's death, the loneliness and isolation of the White House would draw her back to England.

In September 1953 Mary returned to St Kitts with her mother and Daway. In early March the following year Charles made trips to Antigua and Montserrat and back to St Kitts, before returning to England alone at the end of April. He visited Olive, and

took her to see Emmie Bisshopp, the widow of Teddy, Charles's old friend. Charles also made a trip to France.

It was intended that Mary and her mother would follow Charles in early June, but Mary's mother's health deteriorated and she had another operation on her leg, delaying their return to England. Charles's anxieties about protecting his income from the external threats to the cotton and sugar industries, from taxes, and from an imprudent spender, coloured his response to this crisis. He now appeared mean-spirited, not only towards his wife but also his mother-in-law, who had pleaded Charles's cause during Mary's extended trip to Malta and expressed personal admiration for him: 'a most remarkable man, the most unique character I've ever met'. When Mary asked him to authorise an advance on her next instalment of directorship fees – to cover reasonable costs associated with their prolonged stay, medical fees and booking passages back to England for her mother, Daway and herself – Charles felt that he was being exploited and they argued over it in several letters. Mary arrived back at Snowshill in August 1954.

NOT A MUSEUM

Charles's return to Snowshill in 1954 was the first time he had been back in nearly three years. He was concerned at seeing visitors allowed to freely wander throughout the manor and handle what they wanted and noted that, unsurprisingly, 'certain articles have disappeared'. Other houses open to the public showed visitors around in groups and he felt that such an arrangement should be in place at Snowshill.

If items were disappearing from the collection, though, others were being added to it. During this first trip back Charles acquired a further 48 objects for the collection and also accepted his friend Holland-Martin's offer to add his own collection of farm implements to Snowshill, where the Trust suggested they be displayed in the garden houses. Mary told Charles that he had 'made a wonderful collection', but 'I think you should stop now – it is getting overcrowded'. This appeal fell on deaf ears and Charles continued to add to a house and collection that was no longer his.

After acquiring new pieces he would naturally rearrange the collection, which was not well received by the frustrated Maxwell. Maxwell remarked that 'Mr. Wade's presence here is not without embarrassment'; Charles was acting as though the manor was still 'his sole property' and continued to instruct Mr and Mrs Hands to cut wood, light fires and perform numerous other tasks. Charles would speak to people above Maxwell's head, which must have infuriated a man of his status and experience in the museum and gallery sector.

In the years that followed, the Trust struggled to balance the various needs of Snowshill: to preserve its 'spirit of place' and unique identity; to conserve the buildings, garden and collection; to ensure accessibility to visitors physically and intellectually, while also maintaining

it as a viable commercial operation. To the Trust, significantly improving the lighting was critical to providing a successful visitor experience. Charles allowed the addition of a small dormer window at the east end of Hundred Wheels to provide more natural light, but was resistant to reopening blocked windows. Champion of the light of the sun, moon and flame, he expressed his abhorrence of electrical lighting in verse:

> There is a nightmare shop I've seen
> Fluorescent light of ghastly green,
> A horrible shadowless place
> Where everyone has a flat green face,
> As wraith arisen from the tomb,
> In odious shadowless room …

Though resigned to the need for electricity for the manor's new operations, this did not prevent Charles criticising the Trust's careless fluorescent tube lighting. The Trust accepted his criticisms, removing the offending lights and making greater efforts to conceal lighting or convert existing

The colour Wade Blue that Charles felt complemented limestone and garden greens, adorns the Well Court and Sancta Maria.

Above: The manor and cottage as viewed from the apple orchard. *Right:* Snowshill garden today.

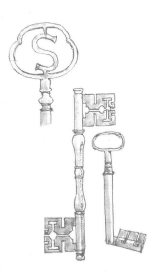

lanterns or candelabras. The addition of electrical lighting did not, however, put an end to visitor complaints that the manor interiors were too dark, and such criticism persists, despite a major refurbishment in 2004.

From the start of Trust ownership it was felt that the manor, due to the size of its collection and its viewing conditions, was not an ideal attraction. Maxwell struggled with the motivations behind the collection and its arrangement. The Trust felt that Snowshill was neither an ancient family seat nor a museum: 'There is little that has value as a work of art, and the interest of the collection lies largely in the fact that it is an expression of an unusual taste and outlook.' Throughout Trust ownership the density of the arrangement not only overwhelmed the aesthetic merits of individual objects but also obscured the architectural merit of the manor interiors. The Trust felt that it could make any changes it thought reasonable and was not obliged to seek Charles's acceptance, although Charles himself always made it clear that the manor was not a museum.

Whilst the Trust had reassured him in 1951 that Snowshill would not be 'labelled as a Museum!', by 1953 Maxwell was recommending in a discussion paper that Snowshill should focus on being a museum of 'local by-gones', costumes and musical instruments. He suggested:

> Two of the large rooms on the ground floor might be cleared and refurbished with suitable furniture using some pieces from other rooms. Is it possible to divert other suitable pieces or to secure some on loan from the Victoria and Albert Museum?

Maxwell felt that the 'theoretical things' (scientific instruments) were 'completely out of keeping' and the oriental collections (including the Samurai armour) should be removed entirely from the property. He was later to go further, stating that 'the house [is] much too full of oddments, at least 50% of which could be eliminated with great advantage'. The Trust's area manager, Colin Jones, agreed that 'a number of knowledgeable people from this district have also made the comment with regard to clutter at Snowshill'. Maxwell thought Charles's plan for the costume cloister and tower was an excellent idea; however, if this could not be achieved, then with the oriental collection removed, the Green Room should display the costume. He believed that it was essential for the Trust to ask Charles what his aim for the manor was.

FINAL YEARS

On 23 September 1954 Charles and Mary, with Daway, returned to St Kitts via Guadeloupe to settle back into their life on the island. Between Guadeloupe and St Kitts they took to the air for the first time in their lives.

By early 1956 they were planning an extended trip back to England. Charles wanted to visit Snowshill and other old haunts, and see family and friends. Mary's mother was increasingly unwell and Mary wanted to spend time with her. Then, three weeks before leaving St Kitts Fred Hart wrote to Charles telling him that Olive, who had been frail for a couple of months, had been hospitalised and was 'dangerously ill' with 'heart trouble'.

Charles and Mary left St Kitts on 23 March 1956, leaving Daway at the White House to maintain the grounds. Prior to their arrival in England they had decided against staying in the cottage in favour of the Lygon Arms. The accommodation here was more to Mary's liking. Although the cottage was her private residence by right, after Charles's death she declined to stay there and let the National Trust open parts of it to the public, reserving her bedroom, Unicorn, to store surplus clothes and personal effects. The reasons for Charles's acquiescence to staying at the Lygon Arms are not hard to imagine. He was 73 and, as his handwriting attests, becoming frail.

Olive survived her bout of illness at this time and went on to live for another two years. However, on this visit to England Charles was diagnosed with cancer of the right bronchus. Given that one of the defining characteristics of his beloved manor was the smell of wood smoke, this

View from the top terrace of the garden towards St Barnabas Church.

is not altogether surprising. Richardson met up with him and learned that Charles was to undergo an operation, but his friend's appearance left him 'doubtful of his expectancy of life'.

Though Charles and Mary succeeded in visiting Italy, Switzerland and France for a month, Charles returned to England suffering with a cold that he could not shake off. It became progressively worse and he was admitted to Evesham Hospital with pneumonia. He never recovered and died there of acute pneumonia on 28 June 1956.

Charles was buried next to Amy and Connie at St Barnabas Church in Snowshill on 2 July. Mary would not join him until more than 40 years later. His obituary in the *Evesham Journal* was headed: 'Death of Mr C P Wade of Snowshill: A True English Eccentric'.

Postscript

On hearing of Charles's death Sir Albert Richardson wrote in his diary:

Alas, that we poor mortals should be so deluded as to imagine we can defeat nature. ... I felt crushed. ... I could write much more concerning him and his kindness to others. He was a gentle soul, refined, thoughtful and austere. Deeply interested in beauty, he could not bear the modern contraptions that young architects of today admire. Alas, we all come to an end. Wade's monument will be Snowshill and the atmosphere he created there.

A self-portrait: a final image of Charles before his death, taken from his last complete notebook.

Snowshill is a remarkable monument. For some Charles Wade's collection is instantly engaging, while others need guidance to unlock the values underlying it and its unusual arrangement.

Charles was a wonderful host and delighted in the pleasure he gave to visitors. He welcomed over ten thousand to Snowshill between 1925 and 1946, and was keen for students in particular to view and learn from his collection. Since 1951 the National Trust has taken up the role of host and, despite different challenges, has endeavoured to follow Charles Wade's approach and keep his spirit alive.

Charles Wade left certain instructions regarding the presentation of the collection; for him this was vital for his storytelling.

He particularly valued the mysterious atmosphere created by candlelight and so, although it is not possible to light the manor with candles today, historic fittings – some from Wade's own collection – have been converted to replicate this characteristic light. It was an important part of the theatre and storytelling for Charles Wade, so it is important to the National Trust.

The National Trust is still learning about Charles and his collection. A detailed study of his notebooks is furthering its understanding of Charles's intentions and aspirations for Snowshill. These discoveries provide the volunteer room guides with authentic details and enchanting stories that would never fit onto any museum label.

The rich variety of Charles Wade's collection means every visit leads to a new discovery, a testament to his unique vision. Ultimately, Charles viewed objects with a different perspective. He not only saw the beauty of the items he collected, he recognised the skills and dedication of the craftsmen and women who created them. Snowshill is his extraordinary tribute to them and their craftsmanship.

The west front of Snowshill Manor painted by Charles.

Select Bibliography

Buchan, W., *John Buchan: A Memoir* (1982)
Freund, P., *Snowshill Manor and Garden Guidebook* (2014)
Hodge, B., *Cotswold born 'n' bred: My Life at Snowshill* (1993)
Jessup, M. (ed.), *Days Far Away, Memories of Charles Paget Wade* (1996)
Mason, C., *Snowshill: A Cotswold Village* (1987)
Miller M. & Gray A.S., *Hampstead Garden Suburb* (1992)
Murray, K., *The Spirit of the House* (1915)
Salwey, J., *Sketching in lead pencil for architects and others* (1926)
'The Ancient Garden of Snowshill Manor House' in *Arts & Decoration* (July 1924)
Tinniswood, A., *Treasures from the National Trust* (2007)

OTHER SOURCES
Charles Paget Wade Papers, Gloucestershire Records Office D10423
Slave Register for St Kitts 1831
St Christopher Gazette and Caribbean Courier
Katherine Blanche Spencer, Journals and letters 1858–1877
Records of the St Kitts Government Archives
Snowshill Manor Archives

View from the Well Court up to the manor house.

Right: A watercolour featuring a procession of historical figures, painted by Charles for *The Strange Adventures of Nemo and Nulla.*
Back cover: Banner of the Duke of Cambridge from his stall at St George's, Windsor.